Metadata Basics for Web Content

The Unification of

Structured Data

and Content

Michael C Andrews

Copyright 2017 Michael C Andrews

ISBN: 9781520553467

Table of Contents

PREFACE — XIV

Why I Wrote This Book — xiv

Why Care about Metadata? — xvii

Who is this Book for? — xx

Coverage Focus: Everyday Web Content — xxiv

How to Use this Book — xxvi
    What's Not Covered — xxix
    How Much Code Do You Need to Know? — xxx

Acknowledgements — xxxiii

CHAPTER 1. INTRODUCTION: WEB TEAMS AND METADATA — 1

Authors and Content Strategists — 5

Designers, Information Architects and UX Specialists — 6

Front-end Developers — 7

SEO Specialists — 8

Analytics Professionals — 9

Data Architects and Enterprise Architects — 10

Business Partners	11
Customers	12
Transcending Silos	13
Taming Terminology	13
Countering Provincialism	14
Creating Team Purpose	15

PART I. THE USES OF METADATA — 17

CHAPTER 2. THE ROLE OF METADATA IN WEB CONTENT — 19

What is Metadata? - A Closer Look	19
Defining Metadata	20
Aliases and Related Terms	20
What Metadata in Web Content Does	23
When Does Web Content Need Metadata?	26
Ways Metadata Makes Web Content More Dynamic	29
Who Benefits from Metadata?	30
Examples of Everyday Web Content Metadata	35
A Content Record	35
A List of Records	37
A "Graph" of Relationships	39

CHAPTER 3. BASIC METADATA ANATOMY — 44

The Basic Building Blocks of Metadata	44
Describing Properties with Metadata.	46

Four Core Metadata Concepts ... 47
   Content Item ... 48
   Relationship of Content Items to Content Types ... 50
   Entity ... 51
   Attribute ... 57
   Values ... 60

CHAPTER 4. METADATA APPLIED: USE CASES ACROSS THE CONTENT LIFECYCLE ... 65

Metadata Makes Content Publication More Manageable ... 65

How Publishers Use Metadata Internally ... 67

How External Distribution Channels Use Metadata ... 72
   Search Engines ... 72
   Social Media ... 76
   Syndication: RSS & Atom ... 77
   Content as a Service: APIs ... 77

CHAPTER 5. METADATA FUNCTIONS ... 82

Metadata Functions and Purposes ... 83
   Administrative Metadata ... 84
   Descriptive Metadata ... 89
   Structural Metadata ... 91
   Rights and Permissions Metadata ... 95
   Technical Metadata ... 105
   Integrated Metadata ... 108

Examples of Metadata as Applied to Content and Media Formats ... 112
   Article metadata ... 112
   Web Media or Digital Asset Metadata ... 113

| Transactional Business Metadata | 115 |

PART II. HOW METADATA WORKS — 117

CHAPTER 6. DATA EXCHANGE STANDARDS / METADATA MARKUP FORMATS — 119

| **Why Markup Matters** | 120 |

XML	123
What XML is	123
When and Why XML is Used	125

HTML Data Formats	129
When and Why HTML Data Formats are Used	129
Microformats	131
Microdata	136
RDFa	141

JSON	148
What JSON is	148
When and Why JSON is used	149
Standard JSON	150
JSON-LD	153

| **Data Standards for Semantic Metadata Compared** | 158 |

| **Syntax Diversity** | 161 |

CHAPTER 7. DATA STRUCTURES, OR METADATA SCHEMAS — 162

| **How Structures or Schemas Supply Meaning to Metadata** | 163 |

Why Data Structures are Important	**166**
The Value of Public Metadata Schemas	167
General Purpose Metadata Schemas	**169**
Schema.org	169
Dublin Core	184
Open Graph Protocol	187
Popular Specialized Schemas	191
Proprietary Schemas	193
Choosing a Schema	**197**

CHAPTER 8. DATA VALUES & CONTROLLED VOCABULARIES 200

Getting the Facts Right	**201**
Ensuring Consistency in Descriptions	**206**
Common Approaches to Text Values	206
How to Develop Common Terminology	211
Using External Controlled Vocabularies	**215**
Widely-used Controlled Vocabularies	216
Special Case: DBpedia	220
Differences Between Audience-facing and Enterprise Taxonomies	**223**
Enterprise Taxonomies	223
Audience-Facing Taxonomies	224
How Enterprise and Audience Taxonomies Differ	226
Reconciling Audience and Enterprise Taxonomy Needs	227
Developing a Propriety Enterprise Taxonomy	**230**
When to Develop Own Taxonomy	230

Costs and Risks of Proprietary Taxonomies	**235**
When External Vocabularies Are Risky	236
Harmonizing Internal Terminology	237
Taxonomies and the Categorization of Content	238

CHAPTER 9. FORMATTING & STANDARDIZING DATA VALUES — 252

A Question of Character	**253**
Why the Format of Data Values Matter	**256**
Consistency	256
Intelligibility to machines	257
Enforcing Value Formats	**262**
Guidelines for Metadata Creators	262
Computer Validation	263
Equating the Audience Description with Computer Values	266
Functionality and Data Formats	**270**
Automation	272
Support of User Experience Functionality	273
Key Public Standards for Data Values	**276**
Languages	277
Dates and Times	278
Postal Addresses	280
Countries	280
Geolocation	281
Telephone Numbers	283
Product IDs	284
Personal Names	285
Music	286

Company names	287
Industry Identifiers	288
Transliteration of Names	289
Units of measure	290
Currencies and Prices	292

Precision and Machine Readability in Descriptions — 295

CHAPTER 10. CLEANING METADATA — 299

Working with Existing Metadata — 300

Why Clean Metadata is Important — 302

   Defining Good and Bad — 302

Poor Governance Can Hurt Metadata Quality — 307

Common Problems in Metadata Quality — 308

   Missing Values — 308
   Inconsistency in Values — 309
   Duplication — 309
   Machine and Human Errors — 310

Approaches to Cleaning Metadata — 314

   Auditing — 314
   Refactoring Metadata — 316
   Ongoing Maintenance — 319

CHAPTER 11. THE FUTURE OF METADATA FOR WEB CONTENT — 321

Web Metadata and Digital Media — 321

Visual Metadata	323
Granular Video	324
Live Content	326

APPENDIX A. APPROACHES TO TURNING METADATA INTO CODE —— 328

Hand Coding	329
Lightweight Markup	330
External Loading of Metadata	331
Graphical Annotation Editors	332
Hardcoded Metadata	333

APPENDIX B. GLOSSARY OF METADATA TERMS —— 334

APPENDIX C. RESOURCES —— 347

Data Exchange Standards	347
Schemas	348
Controlled Vocabularies and Data Formats	349
Useful Books	353
Tools for Cleaning and Validating Metadata	355
Select Metadata-oriented Tools for Developers	356

APPENDIX D. ABOUT THE AUTHOR 357

INDEX 358

"When things have been correctly distinguished,
and the language expressing them has been made accurate,
then decisive judgments are complete."

Liu Xie (ca. 465-522) in *The Literary Mind and the Carving of Dragons,* citing *the Book of Changes*

Metadata Basics for Web Content

Michael C Andrews

Preface

Metadata makes content more useful and enjoyable, and ultimately, valuable. This book is intended for those who work with web content, and want to improve how content is used. It will help you understand the importance of metadata, and how to define and create it.

Why I Wrote This Book

In my work, I need to explain the uses of metadata to different kinds of people ranging from non-technical executives to seasoned software developers. The first challenge is getting people interested in metadata. Mention metadata at a cocktail party, and watch eyes glaze over. Many people consider metadata as boring, as overly technical, or lacking in creative interest. If they've worked with metadata before, they may consider metadata a pain to deal with, because of the time involved creating it, or the seeming complexity it entails. Those familiar with one aspect of metadata may assume they already know everything that's important, and dismiss other approaches that might be useful.

Metadata has a public relations problem. The term is abstract and seems disconnected from our daily lives.[1] Even the most common definition of metadata, that it is "data about data," seems unhelpful and obscure. If metadata were a product vying for attention from buyers, it suffers from poor branding and muddled marketing. It's not obvious to many people what metadata is, and why they need it in their web content. Other people sense metadata matters, but may not have a full sense of its potential.

Metadata is a vitally important issue, and a rich topic as well. I'm not going to pretend metadata is fun, or necessarily simple. It is not always easy to grasp because there are many dimensions to metadata, making it challenging to see how the different dimensions are connected. But understanding how metadata components work as a *system* can clarify how it can influence activities that matter to your organization. Well designed metadata can make life easier both for your customers and for your employees. When the right metadata is in place, people feel that the content they are using "just works".

This book is a survey of how metadata works with everyday web content. It is intentionally broad, seeking to expose you to different topics that could potentially be relevant to your specific work, even if some will not necessarily be so. Web content is diverse in the range of topics it addresses, how it is managed and delivered, and the goals that organizations hope to achieve with it. By providing a survey of the different dimensions of metadata, I hope you can identify what's most relevant to you now, and in the future. What's useful in this book will depend on your existing knowledge, the size and goals of your organization, and the current state of your content operations.

Metadata is a *multidisciplinary* activity, requiring the *collaboration* of people with different backgrounds and responsibilities. One reason I've chosen to present the big picture of metadata is to help promote more collaboration between people in different roles.

The book combines a high-level discussion of core concepts in metadata, together with some details on topics that will be of specific interest to people with different responsibilities. While the survey approach limits the amount of detail that can be covered on each topic, the book provides links to articles, documents and standards that cover these specific issues in deeper detail.

---

[1] How metadata supports web content is not widely understood. If everyday users of digital information read or think about metadata at all, it is most often in the context of metadata relating to personal communications such as emails and phone calls, rather than web content. This leads some people to conclude that metadata is something that compromises privacy and therefore is inherently bad. This book focuses on metadata for published web content, not metadata relating to personal communications. Its emphasis is on how metadata can bring more transparency to publicly available content.

Why Care about Metadata?

Metadata touches nearly everyone who's involved with producing or using online content. If you are concerned about whether your content gets used, then you should be concerned about metadata.

In most organizations, web content plays a vital role in marketing and customer service. Organizations of all types are using digital technologies to run their operations, and depend on web content to communicate with customers. At the same time, they face growing challenges getting the right content to the customers seeking it, and on the right platform where those customers want it.

Web content presents the illusion of simplicity. It seems straightforward to create, and on the surface does not seem nearly as complex as business data. Over time, web content tends to pile up, and becomes harder and harder for organizations to manage, and for customers to use. The reality is that web content is expensive to produce, deliver and maintain. It can be messy to work with, and requires sophisticated information technology (IT) to manage. Yet web content is fundamentally different from the uniform, ordered data managed by most IT systems. It is subject to much more variation.

Web content metadata provides a solution for how people and IT systems can manage the variation intrinsic to web content. It brings greater precision to content, so that organizations can provide exactly the right content to person seeking that content. It is one of the most important factors influencing how content performs: how it reaches audiences, whether it is utilized, and how the impact of content gets measured. Metadata acts as the glue that binds together different items of content, and unites this content with specific people in specific situations.

The well-informed choices that popular on-demand content services like Netflix now offer have raised expectations about how consumers want and expect to get content. Netflix has become celebrated for using over 1000 metadata tags to guide recommendations to their customers. According to one industry report: "It's well known that Netflix invests $150 million per year in its semantic recommendation technology, which covers employing 800 in-house professionals — including 300 content experts who manually tag each and every entertainment title."[2] What seems like magic to consumers can involve extensive detail and planning.[3]

---

[2] Yosi Glick, "Understanding the True Value of Semantic Discovery" *Multichannel News*, June 10, 2015. `http://www.multichannel.com/blog/mcn-guest-blog/understanding-true-value-semantic-discovery/391250`

[3] Netflix is just one example of the trend toward computer-driven content curation. Audiences want content selected based on topics and genres of personal interest. In all kinds of content, such as music and news, audience interests are being

categorized and represented in metadata, to enable computers to curate content for audiences.

Who is this Book for?

To get the most from this book, having a bit of experience dealing with metadata in some capacity will be helpful. This book assumes you have a basic familiarity with some sort of metadata used in web content, and therefore already have some idea what metadata is. The book doesn't assume you know about *all* the areas of metadata, or that you are an expert in metadata.

Perhaps you are an information architect who understands the importance of the categories that users see to find content, but you don't know much about how categories get translated into metadata.

Possibly you are a front end developer who can code some metadata syntax, but you don't know a lot about some of the concepts the syntax represents.

Maybe you are a writer who knows that it is helpful to provide structure to content so that it can be repurposed easily, but you don't know much about how structured writing interacts with metadata.

Perhaps you are an SEO specialist who is very familiar with metadata used by search engines, but are less familiar with other kinds of metadata that affect the management of web content.

Whatever your role, you probably have spent some time using a content management system of some type, even if you don't understand fully how it works.

This book aims to round-out your knowledge of metadata for web content. It won't make you an expert on everything, but it should help fill in your knowledge on topics about which you are less familiar. The goal is to help you discover the different ways metadata can bring value to web content.

Broadly speaking, we can divide metadata stakeholders into three groups:

1. People who design how content is structured so that it can leverage metadata

2. People who create information or data that is stored as metadata

3. People who utilize metadata as an input to other activities.

This book is focused on providing knowledge useful to defining an organization's requirements for metadata.[4] Defining metadata requirements is important anytime your organization does a big web project, such as:

- Redesigning your website so that it can work across different channels

- Upgrading your content management system

- Establishing a new content initiative such as a series of white-papers or podcasts

- Working to integrate content from different websites so that customers don't have to hunt for information they need.

Metadata requirements are also important when you need to improve:

- Your targeting of audience segments you want to reach

- How search engines understand your content

- How your analytics data is showing how effective different content is performing.

Most people who work with web content don't need to become experts on metadata. What's important is that they understand the core concepts and principles, especially as they relate to the detail needed, and how to ensure metadata is high quality. It's important to know what kinds of metadata you need to focus on, since every organization producing online content has different needs. We will look at common applications of metadata, and popular vocabularies used in web content, to help you identify areas that are relevant to your specific situation. Read this book not just to understand, but to get ideas about what metadata concepts and techniques might be beneficial for your entire organization.

[4] Organizations will follow different requirements processes that define the scope and activities for requirements. I am using the term requirements in a generic sense to refer to setting goals for what metadata should accomplish, and identifying tasks that need to be done to achieve those goals. Requirements relating to metadata include business requirements, technical requirements, and user requirements.

Coverage Focus: Everyday Web Content

Metadata can be applied to many types of information. This discussion focuses specifically on everyday web content that will be seen by online audiences, such as customers or viewers of news and entertainment. Those who create and manage content for online audiences have needed an explanation of what they should know about metadata, and this book aims to offer that.

Because this books focuses specifically on metadata for web content, it is not an introduction to metadata in general.[5] Specifically, this book **doesn't address**:

- Metadata for documents, books, or archival collections

- Metadata for personal communications such as email

- Metadata for business data records such as customer, sales and inventory data.

People who work in roles outside the immediate field of web content publishing, such as document, information and knowledge management specialists, business data analysts, librarians, or translators, may find some ideas of value as well, but their needs aren't the focus here.

[5] Readers interested in metadata for other types of content should consult Jeffrey Pomerantz's book *Metadata*.

How to Use this Book

Chapter 1 explores how people working in different job roles can benefit from metadata, and how web teams can collaborate to develop metadata requirements.

The body of the book is structured in two parts. In Part I, four chapters cover high-level concepts needed to understand how metadata works. Chapter 2 introduces what metadata does, and how it works with common types of web content. Chapter 3 covers the anatomy of metadata, which looks at the different components of metadata, and the different terms used to describe these components. Chapter 4 follows with a discussion of different use cases for metadata, giving examples of how metadata might be useful to your organization. Chapter 5 continues the discussion of metadata uses, by considering the five distinct roles metadata can play. This is helpful for those who are only familiar with one or two roles of metadata.

After the discussion of the high level concepts of metadata, we turn in Part II to specific topics associated with metadata requirements. Four key decisions must be made in order for metadata to get implemented in practice:

- What coding syntax will be used for the metadata?

- What organizational schema will be used for the metadata?

- What terms will be used to describe things within the metadata?

- What rules will be used to format metadata values?

A chapter will be devoted to each of these issues, and why they are important. Chapter 6 looks at the coding syntax used to express metadata. This may seem like a dry topic to some, but gaining some familiarity with the different coding syntaxes used will help you understand specific examples in subsequent chapters. Chapter 7 introduces several of the most common metadata schemas that are used to indicate what different metadata fields refer to. Chapter 8 discusses the importance of having a consistent way to describe things, and how controlled vocabularies and taxonomies can help. Chapter 9 addresses how to standardize values used in metadata. If one or more of these topics is new to you, and you aren't sure what they are about, don't worry — they will be described in more extensive detail as each is introduced.

The final two chapters look at other dimensions related to metadata. Chapter 10 looks at the quality of existing metadata, and whether cleaning is required. Chapter 11 considers some areas where current metadata practices for web content are difficult, but where emerging technologies promise significant improvements.

Each chapter begins with a preview section that provides a quick overview of the major concepts in the chapter, and introduces key terminology used. For readers who have no background on a topic, this preview can provide a simple summary of what is important to know about the topic, without being burdened by detail. For readers who are familiar with the topic already, the preview introduces some key terms that will be used in the chapter. Since terminology relating to metadata is far from standardized, I encourage readers to pay close attention to the meaning of terms used in the book, which may differ from other ways the same term, or a similar term, is used in the context of metadata. Often people have trouble understanding a concept because they are already familiar with another concept that is called the same thing, and assume that's what is being discussed.

I've done my best to rely on the most commonly used terminology relating to metadata, and not to introduce my own terms or use nonconventional definitions. But that doesn't mean that how I use terms and definitions will be the same as how you have been using them. Be open to the possibility that there may be many other people who work in the field of metadata who refer to concepts using terminology differently than you do, and use terms you are familiar with in different ways.

Metadata concepts can be very abstract, and challenging to grasp at first. Reading about abstract concepts requires patience, so don't give up if the meaning of a concept is not obvious to you on the first reading.

The book is short enough to read from beginning to end in order to understand the broader landscape, but it also aims to provide enough detail that you will benefit by consulting it again. Some of the content will not necessarily be immediately relevant, so feel free to skim over topics that are not related to your current needs.

What's Not Covered

The book's focus is on metadata *requirements*, providing a foundation to understand such topics as:

- What constitutes quality metadata?
- How can metadata be used?
- What makes metadata complete?

The book **doesn't focus** on metadata *development* — topics such as how to code machine-valid metadata, or detailed discussions of implementation choices. The technical details of metadata markup and structure can involve extensive documentation that's beyond the scope of this book. Detailed documentation is available online relating to metadata markup standards.

This book also **doesn't cover** the mechanics of how metadata works with content management systems or other IT systems such as customer relationship management (CRM) tools. These are important topics, but involve a significant amount of detail that won't be of interest to everyone. Readers interested in those details should consult books and articles on content management systems and associated technology relating to what is called customer experience (CX).[6]

Finally, readers will notice that I shy away from making specific recommendations about choices relating to syntaxes, schemas and controlled vocabularies to use. A core part of a requirements process is to discover what is right for your organization specifically. There is no single best metadata syntax, or single best product taxonomy. There are far too many variables in the kinds of content published, and organizational needs and objectives associated with that content, to recommend a single set of choices that is right for everyone. For those who need a starting point, look at options that are currently most popular, as there can be operational benefits when following conventions widely used by others. But don't limit yourself to choosing only what's popular if it doesn't fit your needs. The field of metadata is undergoing rapid change, so keep an eye on any emerging initiatives that could offer value to your organization.

How Much Code Do You Need to Know?

You can benefit from reading this book even if you know very little about computer code, though you may not understand some details in the book.

While metadata ultimately relies on computer code to work, metadata should not be considered as an exclusively technical discipline. Metadata supports web content, and web content exists for humans to read or watch. Everyone involved with web content needs to be included in discussions about what metadata is needed, as we'll explore in detail in the `Chapter 1`. That includes writers, designers, and those involved with content marketing — individuals who may not have a technical background.

Many important decisions relating to metadata do not depend on understanding coding. And many coding decisions are highly technical, and while critical to successful deployment of metadata, will only be of interest to a small subset of a web team. Metadata code can be lengthy and involve much variation, depending on how it's implemented. Fortunately, tools are improving that let authors add metadata without worrying about the code behind it. A short discussion of how metadata becomes encoded is available in `Appendix A`.

This book won't present much code, but it will illustrate what a snippet of code looks like in some examples, to help demystify what you might encounter. The goal is to help you be able to read a bit of metadata code, rather than teach you how to write it. I've avoided presenting long examples that might be hard to follow, and might distract from the main thrust of the discussion. As a result of this decision, I can't always illustrate every example with a code snippet, since specifying some kinds of metadata requires unusually verbose sequences of code. But the examples provided should offer a general sense of how metadata is encoded.

How to write valid code depends on many factors, and requires a more detailed discussion than can be offered here.[7] The code examples featured are taken from authoritative sources such as standards documentation. A link for each example to these sources is provided in case you want to see a more detailed explanation about the example, and the standard being illustrated. For those interested in actually writing code, the reference linked should provide the necessary details.

---

[6] A good introduction to content management is Deane Barker's book *Web Content Management*.

[7] Occasionally, metadata code that is logically correct does not validate due to some quirk or another. Code can involve many interdependencies. The evolution of metadata standards means that sometimes code that had been working correctly stops working due to changes in a standard, or that new metadata features don't yet work because other software programs haven't caught up. The best information on metadata implementation issues is often found in online discussion forums.

Acknowledgements

I want to thank two reviewers of an early draft of this book, Aaron Bradley in Canada and Joe Pairman in England, who provided helpful feedback and shared their forward-thinking perspectives with me. I want to thank my wife Kathy for her enduring support throughout the process.

Chapter 1. Introduction: Web Teams and Metadata

Effective metadata for web content requires a team effort. Everyone involved with decisions relating to web content also should collaborate to define requirements for the metadata associated with their web content. Ideally, the team developing metadata requirements is the part of the same team responsible for web projects in general, so metadata decisions can be considered together with other web content decisions.

Without comprehensive metadata requirements, publishers end up making patchwork decisions affecting content. They rush to implement solutions without considering the larger goals for the content. Consider some common problems:

- Web analytics that measure the success of specific pages, but don't reveal larger themes about what topics are of greatest interest to which segments

- SEO markup that improves search discovery, but that doesn't help authors decide what kinds of content to create and promote

- Impressive interactive screen designs that users like, but that are hard to update, because they aren't based on a reusable content structure

- Ad-hoc technical solutions created to share content with a business partner, but which later prove difficult to manage and update.

Metadata requirements are important not just to persons responsible for designing the systems that manage and deliver content. They also affect those who need to work with the metadata on a daily basis, as either contributors, or as end-users. The people who contribute metadata details need to see their value, and know how to supply what's needed. The staff in organizations who can benefit from better metadata need to make sure that those designing content templates and systems understand their needs.

Many who work on a web team in a corporation, non-profit or government department, or work at a web agency serving such organizations, are occasionally consulted about metadata-related questions, or are asked to help out on a metadata task. But such ad-hoc involvement is not the same as collaborating to define a comprehensive and jointly owned set of metadata requirements. Developing and implementing a common set of requirements allows teams to coordinate how metadata is created, used, and managed across different areas of responsibility, such as content creation and development, marketing, digital design, and technical implementation.

Strong web teams draw on cross-functional expertise. Some key roles on web teams include:

- Authors and Content Strategists

- Designers, Information Architects and UX (user experience) Specialists
- Front-end Developers
- SEO Specialists
- Analytics Professionals
- Data Architects and Enterprise Architects
- Subject Matter Experts in Business Development, Marketing and Customer Service

You may recognize the kind of work you do listed among the roles above, or you may oversee people responsible for these activities. The discussions in this book can help you identify how metadata relates to your responsibilities, and supports specific objectives you have.

Metadata must also serve the needs of people outside your organization. This is especially challenging since outside parties are rarely directly involved with defining metadata requirements. Metadata requirements should consider the needs of two major outside groups:

- Business Partners
- Customers

For staff with responsibilities for external parties, such as those involved in business development, operations, marketing, and customer care, metadata can improve how these parties interact with your organization. Subject matter experts in these areas should be advocates for the needs of such external parties.

Let's consider how metadata can support people having various goals, both within your organization and outside of it. (See `Figure 1.1`)

Figure 1.1

How Metadata Supports Internal Organizational Stakeholders and Outside Users of Content

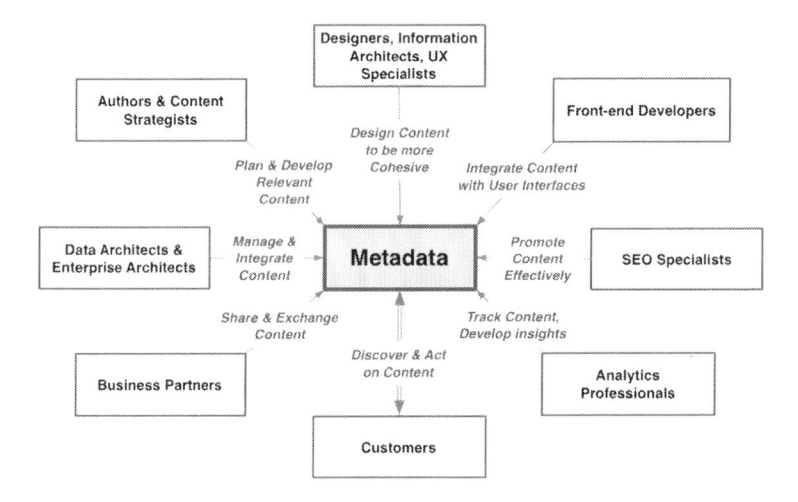

Authors and Content Strategists

The responsibilities of authors and content strategists don't end with planning and creating content. They need to make sure content is used, and that the right content is being created.

Author's Need: Plan, Develop and Leverage Content to be More Helpful

Those involved with planning and developing content increasingly must consider different scenarios for how audiences need content. This involves moving away from generic content, and toward providing content that addresses more specific needs and situations. An understanding of metadata is essential for planning and developing content that is truly relevant to audiences. It enables more precise delivery of content tailored to specific audiences and specific needs.

Designers, Information Architects and UX Specialists

User experience is increasingly linked to content experience. Those involved with helping users need to make sure the designs people use support the content they want to use.

Designer's Need: Design Content to be More Cohesive

People involved with planning and designing how users access and interact with information can benefit from learning more about how content is structured. The containers for content on a screen, and the labels used to navigate through content, need to be tightly tied to content models providing content to the screen. Metadata provides the mechanism to integrate content elements with screen elements. It also allows content to proactively display dynamic messages that can be useful to audiences.

Front-end Developers

Faced with pressures to improve performance speed and interactivity, front-end developers also need to worry about making sure they can manipulate content readily. Front-end developers also must contend with a growing range of devices on which content appears.

Front-End's Need: To Better Integrate Content with User Interfaces to Deliver More Responsive Experiences

Front-end developers work to make interaction a fluid experience. They combine user inputs, on-screen content, and content pulled from servers. As users expect increasingly precise information delivered to often-small screens, front-end developers can benefit from learning more about the breath of content types and elements described with metadata. Metadata can also ensure that content matches the constraints of different devices.

SEO Specialists

Metadata has never been more important to SEO than now. Search engines rely heavily on metadata to locate and display information. Metadata plays an important role in how social media platforms identify content as well.

SEO's Need: Promote Content More Effectively

Search is moving away from finding content, to finding answers. Metadata helps surface answers, and satisfy customer needs more quickly. It attracts audiences to view the content by providing a preview of what's available. Metadata for SEO can't be an afterthought: it needs to work in concert with other goals metadata can support.

Analytics Professionals

Measuring the performance of content keeps growing in importance. Simple measures of the past such as page views are no longer sufficient.[8] Analytics professionals are looking for better approaches to measure business outcomes.

Analytics' Need: Track Content and Develop More Effective Insights

Metadata plays an important role in evaluating content effectiveness and return. Analytics professionals are interested in what metadata indicates about how audiences use content. Metadata provides more a detailed understanding of analytics data, so that outcomes can be linked to and tracked according to topics, formats, timeliness and other dimensions of content. Analytics professionals also need to make sure that business analytics such as customer relationship management (CRM) data are aligned with content metadata.

---

[8] Until recently, many analytics professionals would track audience interest in topics by looking at the words used in the page title or URL, instead using metadata identifying the topic of the content.

Data Architects and Enterprise Architects

Web content is growing in complexity, becoming more modular and involving more diverse media. How to manage it effectively touches on data and enterprise architecture.

Architect's Need: Manage and Integrate Content

IT platforms must be able to integrate content from many sources. They also need to support making content available to many different devices and channels. Architectural decisions can also have a profound impact on downstream capabilities effecting content creation, delivery and tracking. To manage these challenges more effectively, technical architects can benefit from learning more about the audience and business needs shaping metadata requirements.

Business Partners

Business organizations are deepening partnerships to increase operational scale and compete globally. Business partner relationships encompass a growing range of activities including affinity marketing, affiliate marketing, value added reselling, sponsorship, co-branding, service partnerships and outsourcing. Coordinating web content between companies is becoming a critical business issue.

The Business Need: Share and Exchange Content

Business partners are vital for supplying accurate up-to-date information to incorporate in your content, and for providing channels to disseminate content. Metadata enables the automated exchange of content between different organizations.

Customers

Finally, let's discuss the most important stakeholder of all: the customer. It's getting harder to reach customers. They are bombarded with content, and expect the relevance of content to be obvious.

The Customer Need: Discover and Act on Content

Customers care about metadata, even if few know what it is. The most-used websites such as Amazon use metadata extensively to serve customers. The way Google shows snippets and cards highlighting key facts when users search topics is re-setting customer expectations about content: people want instant answers to their questions. Customers have limited time, and want a frictionless experience to get information. Metadata enables that experience.

Transcending Silos

To achieve effectiveness with metadata requires organizations to break down the silos that prevent them from having a comprehensive organization-wide plan of action for metadata. The silos are:

- **Terminology silos**, where different parties can't understand what others are referring to

- **Provincialism**, where different parties only care about their immediate needs for metadata, and not the synergies possible

- The **lack of team purpose**, where different parties aren't on the same page about what metadata is supposed to accomplish

Taming Terminology

Metadata is topic filled with jargon and acronyms. While specialists need to understand a range of terms, the wider team of people involved with creating and delivering web content needs to know how to communicate core concepts with their colleagues, without excessive detail. This book aims to introduce only the most important concepts that will interest a wide range of readers.

The field of metadata has many specialized approaches and variations, so that people with different roles or backgrounds may use different terms and rely on different definitions. Consider the innocent sounding word "entity." To one person an entity is the subject being discussed in the content, but to another person an entity is how a specific character such as the trade mark symbol is encoded. The same situation of divergent meanings exists with other commonly used terms, such as attribute, element and tag. And often individuals will refer to the same concept using different terminology. It is easy to see how people with different specialized knowledge can get confused about what others are talking about.

This book focuses on the common ground in different terminology and definitions, instead of dwelling on distinctions that are largely of concern to specialists. The goal is to help different kinds of stakeholders be able to translate terms and concepts they are already familiar with into terms and concepts other team members know and understand.

This book introduces the core terms you need to know to develop metadata requirements. It allows you to understand the terminology used by your colleagues, so you can speak their language when discussing metadata requirements. A glossary in the appendix provides a set of simple definitions for common terms used when defining metadata requirements.

Countering Provincialism

Individuals may have an excessively narrow view of metadata requirements for different reasons. Sometimes, only one dimension of metadata gets emphasis because that is what gets all the attention from executives. Perhaps someone in marketing is concerned about how content appears in search results, so metadata relating to search engine optimization gets all the focus, and executives assume that metadata and SEO are the same thing. Other times metadata becomes "owned" by a single person because others aren't sufficiently interested in it. Maybe the IT department became the owner of metadata because it is used in the content management system. But web content requires different kinds of metadata, and the IT department may not be in the best position to understand all those requirements.

Metadata can't be someone else's problem. In today's environment, where all kinds of people are involved with creating and delivering content online, it isn't realistic to expect a lone metadata specialist to singlehandedly make metadata work magic. Getting different people in your organization to read this book can help to bridge differences in how people think about the value of metadata.

Creating Team Purpose

The full value of metadata depends on a shared commitment by all stakeholders. A shared commitment means everyone is making sure metadata that's implemented will be good quality and will work well. And it means that everyone is thinking about opportunities to use metadata to support broader business objectives, either by increasing efficiency, improving customer satisfaction, or boosting revenues.

Metadata for web content benefits from a cross-functional perspectives. It requires technical capabilities, methods to link metadata with design and content, the development of vocabularies to describe content, and knowledge of how to apply metadata to all content produced. To implement metadata projects successfully requires resources in all these areas.

Executive sponsors should appreciate that the full benefits of metadata to support the planning, creation, targeting, delivery and evaluation of web content, can be realized only when the full web team is involved with metadata requirements. It can't be achieved with just a few geeks working on their own. Metadata for web content is not just a technical issue: it is a human and organizational one. Executives need to know that the old paradigm of metadata as an entirely technical discipline is dated. True, in the past, only specialized users created or accessed the data described by metadata, and only a handful of people needed to understand the cryptic metadata stored in databases. Today, in this era of web content ubiquity, metadata can't afford to be cryptic. Metadata needs to be relevant. That's why metadata exists: to make content more relevant to audiences.

Various team members can offer unique perspectives about how content can become more relevant, and ideas on how metadata can realize these possibilities. To contribute fully, they need some understanding of what metadata is, and how it works. We'll explore those topics in `Part I`.

Part I. The Uses of Metadata

The first four chapters look broadly at what metadata means in the context of web content. Why is metadata important?

Metadata provides some generic capabilities to web content that are useful to both humans and machines. Metadata is used with web content we encounter everyday, such as articles, product information, and online music communities. Metadata descriptions are based on four key components:

1. What a **content item** is (and what **content type** it is)

2. What **entities** (topics or things) are addressed in the content (and what **entity types** these are)

3. What **attributes** or **properties** are associated with content items or the entities mentioned

4. The **values** for these attributes.

The information specified in metadata can be used internally to support the creation, management and evaluation of content, and externally to enable the content to be delivered through many different channels. Metadata can have different functions. It can:

- Structure content

- Describe what the content is about

- Indicate its history or copyright status, and technical characteristics of content files.

Part I surveys the range of dimensions to consider to develop comprehensive metadata requirements for web content.

Chapter 2. The Role of Metadata in Web Content

Chapter Preview

> Metadata describes a facet or aspect about an item of content, or about a thing identified within an item of content. It is sometimes referred to by other names such as **structured data** or **semantic markup**.
>
> Metadata allows publishers to specify what's in a single item of content, what's in a collection of content, and how different things mentioned in single items or collections of items are related to each other.

What is Metadata? - A Closer Look

Metadata can be both familiar and obscure. Metadata is sometimes exposed and visible to users. Other times is hidden from them.

Consider how people interact with photos. A computer user may have a folder containing photos. The user might see a list of the photo file names, date, and file size of the photo — all metadata elements. Or they may just see thumbnails of the photos, which are organized by date, so that how the metadata is associated with the photo is less obvious. Some really clever metadata software can even automatically tag who or what is in the photo, so that it can tell you what the photo is about.[9]

Intuitively we appreciate that metadata can help us locate and understand content. Metadata has many uses in web content, so let's define what we mean by metadata.

Defining Metadata

There are numerous definitions of metadata, but let's use one that's specifically relevant to web content:

Metadata is data that describes a facet or aspect about an item of content, or about a thing identified within an item of content.

This definition introduces a few concepts or ideas, which we will discuss in detail shortly. It's important to understand metadata as a concept, rather than only through examples. Many individuals have trouble explaining what metadata is exactly, because different examples relate to different dimensions of metadata. We can find numerous examples of metadata used in everyday web content, from the stars customers use to rate a restaurant, to the ability to find a bank branch located near where you currently are. But such isolated examples provide an incomplete impression of what metadata does. Everyone is familiar with metadata from their use of online content, but fewer people understand how metadata is constructed, and what it can accomplish.

Aliases and Related Terms

One confusing aspect of metadata is that some people refer to it by other names. Just because colleagues aren't using the term *metadata* doesn't mean they aren't interested in it. Here are some alternative terms often used to discuss metadata. Notice terms are similar, and be aware of any potential differences in what they might refer to.

Structured Data

Structured data is a term often used by SEO specialists and developers.[10] The term comes from the database world, and refers to the organization of data records. Only more recently has the term been used in association with prose content such as articles. It is largely synonymous with metadata when it describes the subject(s) relating to the content. Structured data sometimes refers to only to descriptions of concise factual data, and not other forms of metadata such as abstracts, or organization dimensions of content such as sidebars. Increasingly, the structured data and metadata are being used interchangeably in forums such as the W3C. We will treat them as equivalent in this book. However, be aware that some developers will consider data in spreadsheets as structured data, even though data structured in spreadsheets do not provide the features typically associated with metadata.

Data fields

People familiar with databases may refer to metadata as the *fields* in a database.

Tags

Some content is described using *tags* that indicate the topic of the content. Such tags are a specific type of metadata, often done informally by readers or users who post their content online, a form of metadata known as a *folksonomy*. The hashtags people use in Twitter is an example. But tags can also refer to other concepts, such as when tags refer to markup in content. For example, people may refer to HTML tags.

Markup & Semantic markup

Metadata is sometimes referred to as *markup*. Markup however refers more broadly to any kind of content encoding, such as HTML, and can indicate presentation as well as meaning. *Semantic markup* is a more specific term relating to content meaning that is broadly equivalent to metadata.

---

[9] Automated visual metadata is discussed in Chapter 11.
[10] *Structured data* should not be confused with a similar-sounding term known as *structured content*. These terms are used by different communities to refer to different dimensions of content. Structured content is used by writers and content specialists to refer to the development of standardized document structures. Structured content refers to the organizational structure within articles, videos or other content (e.g., the sequence or conceptual ordering of content sections), rather than to the people, places or things mentioned within items of content. Structured content deals with how content is pieced together, while structured data deals with what is discussed in the content.

What Metadata in Web Content Does

Metadata for web content has a different character than other kinds of metadata used in information technology. Web content metadata is more varied in what it addresses, and how it communicates and interacts with information, people, and IT systems. This variety reflects the diverse uses of web content metadata.

Computer metadata started gaining prominence in the 1980s, before the emergence of web content in the 1990s. As a result, the original focus of metadata was different than today's. Librarians who cataloged books and other physical media needed metadata when transferring their catalog records to computer databases. Around the same time, databases for business operations became widespread. The original focus of metadata was to support the creation of databases — to support cataloging and records management. Originally metadata was largely about housekeeping: filing facts for retrieval later.

Web content, however, is more varied than a list of facts that requires filing.

How does metadata relate to web content? Metadata is not identical to the content, nor it is not something completely separate from it either. Metadata sometimes provides additional information to what's mentioned in the web content, while other times it repeats the same information but in a different form. Some web content won't have metadata associated with it, because metadata may be selective about what it covers. In short, metadata can either *add information* to the content, *clarify information* in the content, or it can *ignore something* in the content.

Metadata is a kind of commentary about the web content. Some of this commentary is created for the benefit of readers, and some of it is made for benefit of machines. Let's consider some ways metadata comments on content.

- **Annotation to explain more**. Metadata provides a form of digital annotation of content that explains different content dimensions and connections. For example, you might read a news story about a company, and find you can view that company's stock price by hovering over the name of the company, with the metadata enabling the display of an extra layer of information.

- **Statement of explicit meaning.** Publishers use metadata to represent the meaning of the content so that computers can interpret the content correctly. Metadata allows computers to find all articles about a topic such as basketball, even if the word basketball is not explicitly mentioned in these articles.[11]

- **Supplemental information for machines.** Metadata offers a reflection of content that supplements the information in the primary (visible) content that audiences view or use. For example, publishers add computer metadata to indicate precisely what the date mentioned in the text refers to. Readers may see the date in the text as "July 11" and know what year is being referred to, while the metadata indicates the date as 2017-07-11, so that the year is also indicated.

- **Structured information for readers.** Metadata sometimes provides information about the content added for humans to read and evaluate. Such metadata might "pull out" key bits of information within content into a separate section that provides descriptive labels next to key information, such as when Wikipedia articles have a fact box that pulls out key facts from the article. This structuring of information can help audiences scan and comprehend the content, and can also enable the content to be more interactive.

Content designers sometimes say metadata brings intelligence to content. Metadata gives pieces of content the ability to converse: to interact with computer instructions, and to coordinate with other pieces of content. Unlike in the early years of computer metadata centered on static records recording past events, metadata today plays an more active role in shaping the online experience of audiences. Metadata is ingredient determining how content is delivered dynamically, according to specific criteria in a given situation. Content metadata allows different configurations of web content, and provides capabilities that let the audience gain control over what they view.

When Does Web Content Need Metadata?

Metadata descriptions highlight the *elements* within web content that publishers consider important to *manage* or *measure*. Metadata provides structure to web content.

IT specialists sometimes refer to the web content people view each day as "unstructured data." The various articles, videos and audio clips we use are stored and delivered by computers, and thus are data.[12] But the computers don't know what the content is about because it lacks a structure computers understand. The content's not segmented into distinct identified elements. Metadata lets computers identify and understand every piece of important information associated with the content. Computers rely on structured data, but the purpose of structuring is not simply to please computers. The ultimate beneficiaries of structure are people, the readers and viewers of online content, who can access the content in flexible ways as a result of the structure that's been defined.[13]

At its most basic, metadata identifies aspects of content that are important, and indicates what that importance is.

1. **Identifying Distinct Elements in Content**.

Different dimensions or characteristics of content have special importance to either the producer of the content, or the users of the content. We can refer to these aspects as elements. Identifying these elements helps ensure that the intentions of the content creator are understood by audiences who access content through digital interfaces. For example, when a date is displayed, it often needs a label beside it to clarify what the date refers to, such as whether it is a start date or an end date.

2. Organizing Elements Through Structure.

Once the important characteristics are identified, these elements need to be organized to show how they fit in the larger context addressed by the content. That context is defined in a formal structure, which indicates the relationship between different content elements. These relationships allow different content elements to be linked or presented together.

The structured elements become discrete components that can be used in flexible ways to deliver content. For example, a publisher might reuse a structured element that provides generic background information, placing it in several articles where it would relevant. The publisher could choose to only use this generic background element in specific variations of each article, perhaps a longer version that provides comprehensive details, and choose to exclude it from the shorter version of the article.

Let's look at some situations where metadata can add value by providing more structure to the content. Metadata can be useful when there's:

- **Visible Information That's Unstructured**. Some information in web content is obvious to humans, but not to computers. Readers can see that an article is written by Jane Bloggs, but computers can't differentiate that text from all the other text in the article, because the author's name hasn't been structured into a distinct element that's been identified so that the computer understands the name refers to the property of author.

- **Poorly Segmented Information**. When metadata is added to information, it can highlight the underlying structure of the content to audiences and make the content more usable. Sometimes how the published content is structured is less than ideal. For example, content might indicate a location by stating the city and state together, without specifying which word(s) represents the city and which represents the state. But when city and state are segmented separately in metadata, it becomes easier to group locations by either city name or state name.

- **Information Whose Meaning is Implicit and Dependent on Context.** Language can be ambiguous. Suppose an article mentions a company named "Johnson". Several companies use Johnson in their name, so which is being discussed?[14] Humans are capable of inferring the meaning of words or phrases based the context, or their prior knowledge of what the content addresses. These are implicit meanings. Metadata makes the meaning more explicit.

- **Invisible Information Computers Can Use**. Some information may be useful for managing and delivering content, but is not information audiences need to see. An example is when metadata records, in the background, the number of views an article receives, which can be used to prioritize the order that articles are displayed. Because only computers see such information, it is sometimes not collected at all, because organizations don't recognize the utility of such information. Metadata can give computers contextual knowledge about content so that it is more relevant and up-to-date.

Ways Metadata Makes Web Content More Dynamic

When computers are able to interpret content elements, a range of applications becomes possible. Metadata can enable web content to have dynamic functionality that's not present in static web pages.[15]

Metadata can support three core content tasks:

1. **Exploring Content**.

    Metadata helps audiences locate content by improving the precision of search. It lets audiences filter content according to different criteria, and lets them verify that the items they are viewing are what they presume them to be.

2. **Explaining Content**.

Metadata useful for understanding a large body of content. It can classify features of the content, providing an overview of the content. It can summarize the content according to topics, and can quantify the number items that relate to an author or time period, and rank items according to their detail or newness.

3. **Customizing Content**.

Metadata can be combined with rules to change what content is displayed according in different situations.

Who Benefits from Metadata?

Who benefits from metadata may not be immediately obvious, because metadata works behind the scenes. Yet a diverse range of actors depend on metadata. It improves the interaction between authors and audiences. It provides a common language to describe what content means that is understandable to content creators, content consumers, and the computer platforms that serve both.

The Human Side of Metadata

People interact with metadata directly to accomplish tasks. They look for metadata on their computer screens that can help them locate the content they need. Metadata is important for both the creators and consumers of content.

- **Authors and Other Content Creators.** Metadata can support the online author experience – it makes creating web content easier to do. Authors use metadata to locate existing content elements to include in the content they create, so they can reuse such elements. Metadata can help automate various tasks such as archiving old content. Authors and editors rely on metadata to let them know how their content is performing – for example, to find out who wrote the most viewed article last week.

- **Readers.** Metadata provides online audiences with a richer experience. Metadata enables filters that can prioritize content according to which facets are most important to them, such as when people filter choices on an ecommerce site. Metadata also supports smarter delivery of content that can anticipate needs instead of only reacting to requests made explicitly.

What is the relationship of metadata to the information architecture of a website or app that's seen by audiences? Metadata and information architecture are complementary but different. Information architecture concerns how to present information to users so that they can understand what the information is about, and locate the information they need. Information architecture depends on metadata. Information architecture is the public face of metadata that's visible – it's how people will encounter metadata when they see it.[16]

Machines as Users of Metadata

A major motivation for metadata is to enable machines to understand the precise meaning of content that has been designed for humans. While humans can infer the meaning of words and phrases based on context and prior knowledge, computers can become confused about what a word refers to. Metadata can eliminate the ambiguity in spoken and written language, or in images and video, and enable computers to interpret the meaning of the context. Many IT systems depend on metadata, but two important ones are content management systems and search engines.

- **Content Management Systems**. Content Management Systems (CMSs) rely on metadata to assemble content that is viewed by audiences.[17] Metadata is especially important for a CMS when providing personalized content based on the user's profile and behavior. Metadata also enables CMS workflow management and automation.

- **Search Engines**. Search engines use metadata to index content to help audiences locate what's most relevant. Semantic search uses metadata to extract information from content, so audiences see key highlights before viewing the full content.[18] Semantic search can also associate content with related content.

[11] Readers can understand the broad topic of sports articles from the context and terms used, such team and player names and lingo such as baskets and dunks. Computers need more explicit guidance to interpret the content.

[12] From an IT perspective, any content stored as a computer file is data. Data in this sense is much broader than statistical data.

[13] When metadata is seen exclusively as an IT issue, some critics will view metadata as just being extra work that needs to be done because existing IT systems are too dumb to understand language. This view has prompted the championing of Natural Language Processing (NLP) as the answer to unstructured data. While NLP has a role to play in developing metadata, NLP by itself doesn't provide structure to content, and is thus limited in how it can help to support audience and publisher needs in different scenarios.

[14] Examples of U.S. companies with Johnson in their name include Johnson & Johnson (*healthcare products*), S.C. Johnson & Son (*wax*), and Johnson Controls (*industrial equipment*).

[15] Much online content is static — presenting the exact same content regardless of who is accessing it, when or where it is being accessed, or what device is being used to access it. When using metadata, content does not need to be frozen at the time it is created. Instead, the content displayed can change dynamically according to a range of criteria identified within the metadata. How metadata can be used to support automation and interactive functionality will be discussed in Chapter 9.

[16] The relationship between information architecture and metadata values will be discussed in greater detail during the discussion of taxonomies in Chapter 8.

[17] Supporting the assembly of content is among the most important roles that metadata plays in a CMS, but is far from

the only one. Metadata supports management of access and security, scheduling content for automated publishing, flagging content for translation, and removing content that is no longer needed.

[18] Semantic search identifies the concepts (expressed in metadata) mentioned in content, in contrast to text-based search, which matches specific keywords in the content with search terms used by the searcher.

Examples of Everyday Web Content Metadata

Examples are the best way to appreciate the varied roles of metadata. Many kinds of web content have a regular structure. Looking at these structures provides a good opportunity to see metadata at work.

Let's look at how metadata figures in three common structures:

1. A content record
2. A list of records
3. A graph of relationships

A Content Record

Content records are not much different from standard database records available in office applications, except that they are specifically designed for non-specialists to read and use, and they may contain a richer range of media. We encounter records when we fill out a form online. The fields have associated values we must fill in, and the entire form represents a single record. Much content involves structured data like this that is stored in a database.

Example of a Content Record: Product Description in Online Catalog

A common example of a content record is a web page that describes a single product within an online catalog for an e-commerce site. The description is composed of many elements. Labels indicate fields of information, which have values associated with them.

Common elements for a product description (*the content record*) in an online catalog include:

- Product title
- Photo
- Manufacturer
- Description of product highlights or benefits (*bulleted list*)
- Model number
- Product features
- Price
- Weight
- Size dimensions
- Warranty
- Product ID number
- Stock availability
- Price.

The product description is composed of many different types of data, from text, to photos, to numeric data about prices and physical measurements. Some records might include a video as well. Another important feature of product descriptions is that the structure of the description might vary. Some products will require additional information, and some standard information such as features may occasionally not be relevant.

How often the values are updated is another variation. Some elements such as model number and product ID will always stay the same. Price will change from time to time, and may vary according to location, while stock availability will change often.[19] The likelihood of change is an important factor when deciding how to manage different content elements.

A List of Records

A *list of records* is similar to the rows and columns in a spreadsheet. Each row represents a separate record, while each column is a characteristic relating to the item described by the record. The column header is equivalent to the label used for each field of a record. (See `Figure 2.1`) Like a spreadsheet, metadata can organize information into a hierarchy, where individual records can be collected together, combined, and summarized.

Figure 2.1

Relationship of Elements in a Record to Elements in a Table

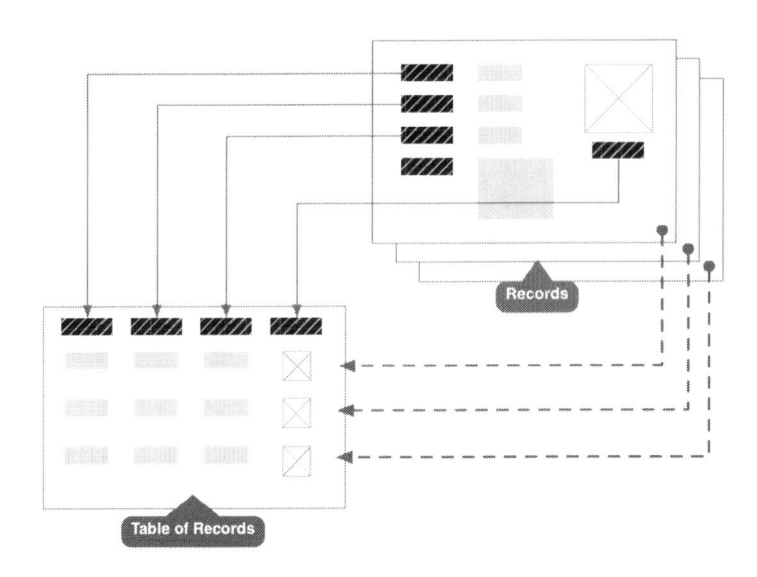

Example of a List of Records: **Table of Product Information**

Let's imagine a table of product information, based on the product descriptions. Such a table allows customers to compare different aspects of products.

While a table of product information will reuse content contained in individual records of product information, there are constraints on how content from the records can be reused and repurposed. To compare different products effectively, all the products should have information relating to same fields. The elements presented in the table should reflect what information audiences want to compare.

Model name and price are obvious elements to include, but not all the elements are going to fit in the table, nor are they all elements audiences will want to compare. Selecting specific elements to include will depend on what common goals users have when assessing the information.

When putting data into table, the data characteristics become important. Consider the possibility that users may want to filter the list. If the product features are written in a paragraph, users can't filter the feature descriptions to locate specific feature categories and values. To enable the filtering of elements, the elements need to be structured in the master record that appears in the full product description. Another element presents a challenge: the photo of the product. We want the photo in the table, but the photo from the full product description is too big. This introduces a new wrinkle requiring metadata: the need for two variants of an item of content, a small-sized and large-sized photo, and the ability to distinguish between the two variants.[20]

A "Graph" of Relationships

In mathematics, a *graph* is a structure that represents relationships and connections between two variables. Metadata that links together and reveal relationships between different things is also known as a graph. Graphs answer how one item is related to another item.

Graphs can be applied to many kinds of content, and are especially prominent in social media. In social media, graphs reveal how the audience is relating to some characteristic of the content. For example, what kinds of content does a person like, or share with others?

Most recently various IT companies including Google have been offering something called *knowledge graphs*. In knowledge graphs, different items can be linked together to create a chain of relationships between items. For example, a graph can answer a trivia question such as in what country were the most Nobel laureates in literature born? To answer such a question, the knowledge graph links together different pieces of information: a listing of names of winners of the Nobel prize in literature, and a list of in what countries those individuals were born.

Digging Deeper: The Bare Basics of Graphs

For many people, the use of the term *graph* to refer to something other than a numeric chart may seem unfamiliar.[21] But the concept of graphs is starting to become more common in web-related discussions. People who work with web content are likely here the terms social graph or knowledge graph, either from technically inclined colleagues, or in the press.

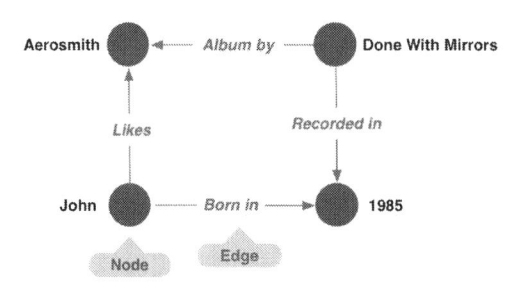

Graphs are composed of *nodes* and *edges*. The nodes represent things and values. These are connected by edges that represent the relationship between the nodes. Conceptually, graphs look a bit like a construction toy that can connect together into ever-larger structures. Graphs can be a powerful way to explore information, but using them depends on having the right information available as metadata, and making sure that information is accurate and reliable.

Example of a Graph: A Social Music Platform

Many forms of content include a social media component. Streaming music services, for example, may incorporate social networking functionality to enhance the listening experience.

A streaming music service will use metadata to follow how a listener interacts with a song. The service will track actions the listener performs in relation to a song, such as when a person listened to a song, or skipped a song, added it to a play list, or favorited it.

Metadata can capture data about three broad categories of variables: music (songs), listeners, and various user actions or behaviors. Behaviors can generate new content, such as playlists or a list of favorites that are derived from the songs played most often. Songs and listeners both have facets that can generate graph associations. Listeners have friends, and may share characteristics with other listeners such as location. Performances of songs have bands, genres and individual performers. These facets can be associated with each other in various combinations. Friends can see a listener's play list. The listener can discover other music by the same band, or involving the same performers. Anyone can learn what band is currently most often played. The ability to make these connections depends on having metadata that describes these facets.

[19] Not only might the base price change according to where the user is located according to the logic of "dynamic pricing", but the currency used to display the price might change as well. Prices demonstrate clearly how metadata can represent variables in content.

[20] Using metadata to swap out different variants of content is known as *conditionality*. Conditional text, for example, could change according to user characteristics (audience segment, location, etc.) or product characteristics (specific features of the product that need to be described in a customized way).

[21] If it helps, one way to think about any kind of graph is that it shows a series of points that are connected by a line or lines. Information flows along the line between each point.

Chapter 3. Basic Metadata Anatomy

CHAPTER PREVIEW

> Metadata is composed of four major parts. The **content item** has characteristics that can be described by metadata, such as the author or date of publication. Content items also typically discuss specific things or topics, which are referred to as **entities**. Each entity (thing mentioned in the content) can be described according **attributes** or **properties** typically associated with the entity. For example, if an article (*content item*) discusses laptop computers (*an entity*), the content might mention different attributes of laptop computers, such as their make or prices, that could be specified in metadata. Every attribute of an entity or content item will need to have a **value** associated with it. If the content discusses the makes (*an attribute*) of laptop computers (*the entity*), then the values will be the names of specific makes mentioned, such as HP or Apple.

The Basic Building Blocks of Metadata

Metadata is composed of building blocks that work as a system to organize information relating to content. The system addresses different levels of detail.

Computers require that content be broken down into uniquely identifiable pieces. For computers to interpret what these pieces mean, they need to know how they relate to each other.

Metadata Provides Frameworks. Like humans, computers need a framework in order to interpret the meaning of items. People rely on mental models to understand the world, based on their experience. Computers need humans to build a model to explain how different dimensions fit together. These models are sometimes called *schemas*. Metadata can build of model to describe how documents are constructed and may vary. They can build models to describe a domain of knowledge, such as medicine or geography. These frameworks involve a hierarchy or a graph connecting different dimensions to form a larger picture. Importantly, the framework enables all computers to have a shared understanding of the meaning, so that they all interpret the meaning in the same way.

Metadata Specifies Details. How much detail is enough? What specific characteristics about the content do you want to identify in metadata? Creating metadata involves making choices about what things to describe, and at what level of detail to describe them. The metadata needs to break down all the information into granular elements that software can process.

Metadata Highlights Associations. How do the details about one thing relate to details about another? Here we are interested in lateral or associative relationships. Audiences might be interested in exploring different relationships between two topics that are not directly related, such as industry sector and a geographic area. Metadata can provide hooks to allow such associations to be made.

Describing Properties with Metadata.

The properties in and about the content need description. The description supplies the specific information indicating exactly what is meant. It's important that the description be consistent. Properties are governed by rules concerning how they are represented.

> **Values**. There can be more than one way to describe what's in the content. Is the content about a car, or an automobile? Designers of metadata should indicate the preferred terms to describe things.
>
> **Formatting of Values**. How do you write dates or numbers? Just as humans need for content to be legible, computers need clearly written values they can understand.

Encoding Metadata

The concepts expressed though metadata need to be encoded in a way that computers can reliably process, into what's called a *machine-readable* format. Different kinds of computer markup are used to encode metadata. These follow specific syntaxes, or rules to express the meaning of the information.

Four Core Metadata Concepts

Four core concepts form the backbone of metadata descriptions:

- Content item
- Entity
- Attributes
- Values.

These four concepts are interdependent, moving from general to specific details.

Discussions of metadata sometimes use differing terminology. Some alternative terms relating to these concepts will be introduced as well, so that everyone involved with web content can understand the common principles and be able to use a shared terminology.

Figure 3.1 shows how the core concepts relate to one another.

Figure 3.1

Relationship Between Different Levels of Description in Metadata

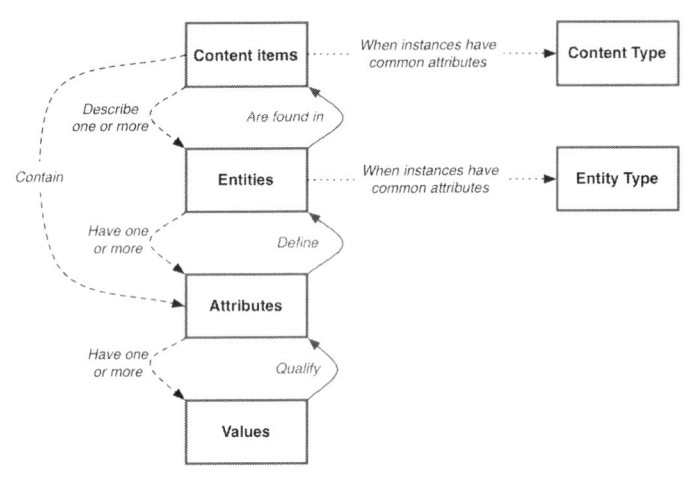

Content Item

Let's discuss what's meant by content. Traditionally content was a document or article, but the range of content items people encounter online has become quite diverse.

What the Term *Content Item* Refers to

A content item is any piece of content that can be used independently on its own, and has meaning for audiences. A content item could be:

- An article
- A video
- A photo
- A map

- An event notice
- A page of product details
- An interactive widget
- A notification
- A form
- A table
- An infographic.[22]

A content item reflects a coherent unit of content that has meaning to audiences on its own. A paragraph within an article would not be a content item since it would not presented independently of the article.[23] However, a paragraph-long notification sent to a mobile device would be a content type, since the notification is a recurring, standalone type of content.

Unlike a paragraph in an article, a content item will often have a title associated with it, though is not mandatory.

Several content items can be combined into a compound item of content. For example, it is common to embedded one item of content within another, such as including a bio of an individual at the end of an article. When items can be understood independently of context, they can become modular components that can be combined in different configurations.

Alternate Names for Content Items

These terms are related to the concept of content items. Both terms, however, may refer to intermediate (unedited or unprocessed) content, rather than to the final version of a content item that is delivered to audiences to view. When discussing the content available to audiences, teams should be mindful of the distinction between what content audiences *could* see (in some version) verses what they *will* see.

Content Assets

Content assets suggests content items (such as a photo) that can be used multiple times for different purposes. The term *digital assets* typically refers to non-text content (primarily photos and video) that is available in a repository for re-use.

Content Objects

A *content object* can refer to a content item in the context of a content management system.

Relationship of Content Items to Content Types

Content items that share a common structure belong to a common content type. A content type is a technical term that is used in different ways. The following definition notes that content types are a *logical* categorization of content: "A content type is a logical grouping of content based on the essence of that content".[24] For example, all content items that describe product details may belong to a product details page content type because all these pages share a common structure. All the product details pages share a common purpose: to convey detailed information about products to customers.

Some content types are closely associated with a delivery format or channel, because the medium defines how audiences receive the content. A podcast is generally associated with audio formats, for example. But content types are not the same as media formats. An interview can be a content type based on a common structure that exists in several formats: as a transcript, as a video, and as an audio. Interviews might have thematic segments that follow a regular structure, and each segment might exist in different formats that could be packaged together or distributed separately.

Entity

The term *entity* is unfortunately a rather abstract word, and may therefore cause some confusion. Lawyers, for example, talk about legal entities, which could be a shell corporation associated with post office box in Delaware, created to disguise who is the real owner is. When we talk about entities in metadata, we are trying to do the opposite: to make it clear who or what is being discussed.

Entities describe people, places and other things mentioned within content items. Narrative content such as articles and videos typically contains descriptive verbal statements relating to identifiable things. The statements provide information about characteristics of an entity that's being discussed. Entity metadata identifies the topic being discussed and maps the specific characteristics mentioned into structured data. For example, we may have an content item that provides travel advice. The content may read: "Visiting Rome in August is not recommended, as it is hot and full of tourists. Its historical sites are best seen in the Autumn and Spring." In this example, the entity being discussed is Rome, Italy (and not Rome, Georgia, USA.)

What the term *Entity* refers to

Let's get more explicit about what an entity is in the context of web content metadata. An entity is a specific *person*, *place*, *date*, *thing*, or *concept* that is described in a content item.[25] Entities are the important topics present in the content. Not everything mentioned in the content will deserve entity metadata. Entities are most valuable when identifying them is important to the audience, because they are significant to the context of things discussed in the content, or to things in other related content.

Entities are generally nouns. Entities are often *proper nouns* that are capitalized in English, since the reference is to a specific thing. But entities can also be a *category* of thing, such as a camera or a tomato, even though there are specific kinds of these entities. Verbal nouns or *gerunds representing activities* such as biking or cooking can also be entities. A less common kind of entity represents *actions* such as to listen, watch or delete, where well-defined parameters might be tracked in relation to the action.[26]

Alternate Names for Entities

Entities are often mentioned in the context of narrative content. The task of metadata is to identify the specific entities that are mentioned in a text or audio recording, or represented in a video or photo. Since entity is a formal phrase, the concept is often referred to by more informal names.

Items Referenced

Items referenced may refer to specific entities such as an event. Items can generally be quantified.

Things Discussed

Things discussed may refer to collective entities, such as a breed of a dog.

Topics

Entities are *topics* that are mentioned specifically in the content. But topics can sometimes refer to a higher-level description that refers to more than one entity, and in such cases are not references to entities, but a summary description. Within the technical writing community, topics are a generic content type used to explain information.[27]

Entity Characteristics are Defined by Entity Types

When different entities can share common features, they belong to the same entity type. (Yes, I know by appending the word *type* to the word *entity*, I've just doubled the level of abstraction. Sorry, but that's the term used by the metadata community. Hang in there.)

It is common to group entities into types, to identify an entity as a person, place, a product, event or organization. Let's consider an entity: Cambridge. At this point we don't know what kind of entity it is. Is it a **Place** entity type, or an **Organization** entity type? Once we identify the entity Cambridge as belonging to the organization entity type, we know that we are not referring to city of Cambridge, Massachusetts, or the city of Cambridge, England. Instead, we are referring to an organization called Cambridge; in this case, Cambridge University. We say that Cambridge University belongs to the entity type called Organization— the general type used to describe things that have similar characteristics. Alternatively, we can say that Cambridge University is an *instance* (specific single example) of the Organization entity type.

It is also possible to break entity types into *subtypes*, so that one has different types of persons, types of products, types of events, or types of organizations. These grouping help to identify and manage specific information relating to entities. In the example of Cambridge University, we identified it as belonging to the Organization entity type, but we also have additional options. The Organization entity type might have subtypes. We could identify

Cambridge University has belonging to the **Educational Organization** entity type. Doing so would allow us to indicate some more specific characteristics relating to Cambridge University in our metadata, such as alumni. We could even get more specific and identify Cambridge University as belonging to the **College or University** entity type.

While entity types are often straightforward, they sometimes present challenges. Be aware that a few people refer to entity types by other names. A *class* or *domain* is a more formal phrase to indicate the type of entity and the characteristics associated with it.

Choosing the right entity type can sometimes be difficult. First, there is the issue of choosing the "best" entity type to capture the right level of detail. Second, an entity instance can belong to more than one entity type, making it difficult to know which entity type the instance belongs to. For example, if a wellness spa offers a particular medical treatment to improve nutrition, that treatment might belong to both the **Service** entity type covering services for sale, and the **Medical Treatment** entity type covering medical interventions.

Examples of Entities and Entity Types

A hypothetical example will illustrate the relationship between entity instances and entity types. It will illustrate how choosing an entity type affects the metadata description.

The **iPhone** (*entity*) is a type of **Smartphone** (*entity type*). All iPhone models share characteristics that are common to smartphones in general, which includes other makes and models. We would indicate the entity type as smartphone and indicate the model name of the smartphone as "iPhone."[28] The smartphone entity type might include characteristics relating to features unique to smartphones such as processor or screen size and resolution.

A **Smartphone** (*entity type*) is a type of **Product** (*entity type*). Some entity types such as smartphone are very specific, while others such a product more more general.

Alternatively we could indicate that an iPhone belongs to the Product entity type. A more general entity is sometimes sufficient to describe the most important aspects. Smartphones have characteristics shared by other products, such as model names, prices, warrantees, and so forth.

Perhaps you are wondering how the boundaries around entity types are drawn. When does the variation among the entities described by an entity type merit the creation of a new, more specific entity type? The answer to that question depends on how much detail is useful and necessary to capture in metadata, and the desire of standards organizations to support more specific entity types. Standards bodies often resist introducing new entity types until there is widespread demand for them, since the complexity increases as more entity types are available for use.

Attribute

If entities identify what something *is*, attributes identify what something *is like*. Attributes provide the description. Attributes allow audiences to compare how similar or different various entities are.

What the Term *Attribute* Refers to

Attributes define the parameters of an entity, and qualify its characteristics. An attribute describes a specific aspect or dimension of either a content item, or an entity mentioned in a content item. It can identify something specific, and indicate what is unique or significant about the content or entity.

There are literally thousands of commonly used attributes we encounter. The attributes used will depend on the type of content or entity being described. For example, IMDb, the popular movie database, lists dozens of attributes for a film, including title, genre, rating, length, release date, director, writers, cast, filming location, and so on.

Entities have various characteristics. Attributes classify the type of characteristic associated with an entity. Returning to the smartphone example, the smartphone has a price, which is an attribute of the smartphone. In conversation, entities are often directly described in terms of their values, without necessarily explicitly saying the kind of value mentioned.

This is especially true for familiar objects such as cars. For example, we might say that a car:

- *Is* red (attribute: **color**)
- *Is owned* by Mary (attribute: **owner**)
- *Was made* in 2015 (attribute: **model year**)
- *Has* good *fuel economy* (attribute: **fuel economy rating**), or
- *Is a* convertible (attribute: **roof variation**).

These relational verbs are translated into formal attributes, so that similar characteristics can be compared across different entities.

Alternate names for Attributes

Attributes is a term a well understood by most content producers, and it a familiar term for developers working with HTML. HTML has attributes, although they don't always indicate metadata, such as when HTML attributes indicate classes for CSS styling.

There are other terms that are similar in meaning to attributes you might encounter.

> Properties

Properties are another way of expressing attributes. Semantic search specialists commonly use the term. Properties refer to the attributes of an identified entity.

Key

An attribute in a database may be referred to as a *key*. It is generally used in the phrase *key-value pair*.

Descriptors/Labels

Descriptors and *labels* are terms used informally to how attributes might appear on a user's screen. Since these terms can refer to other concepts as well, attribute is a more precise term to use.

Kinds of Attributes

Attributes can be quite diverse in how they describe entities. Various kinds of attributes serve different purposes.

- **Concrete Attributes**. Concrete attributes are objective attributes of the content or entity, such as the year of birth, the weight of a product, or author of an item of content.

- **Abstract Attributes**. Abstract attributes are explicitly defined subjective statements about content or an entity, such as the style of music, or genre of a film. Although subjective, abstract attributes rely on people having a shared understanding of the meaning of an abstract concept.

- **Identity Attributes**. Identity attributes are properties that are assigned to a content item or entity to track it, such as an ID number or a title.

- **Hybrid Attributes**. Hybrid attributes are verbal descriptions that present many ideas within a single attribute, such as field for a summary or a short description.

Values

Attributes have values. The value of an attribute answers:

- **What** something is
- **Which one** something is
- **How much** something is.

A value is a name or quantity assigned to an attribute of an entity or content item. It is important to keep in mind that a value, when used in metadata, does not only refer to numeric values. Values can be *text values* representing names and descriptions, and they can also be *dates*, *geographic coordinates*, and even *URL* website addresses.

How values are represented in metadata may differ from how they are presented on a user's screen. When audiences encounter values in content online, they may see stars rating a product, or a photo of blue dress denoting the style and color values associated with product.

What the Term Values Refers To

The value provides the description. For example, we say in conversation "a blue dress," the value blue supplies an identifying characteristic, while the attribute (color) is implied.

It is important however, to associate the value with the appropriate attribute, because values can be applied to many attributes. A complex object like a suitcase might not have a single color value. One may need to identify the suitcase body as red, and the suitcase handle as brown. Values indicate variables — the scope that a description can differ.

There are three main kinds of values: *categories*, *quantities*, and *names*.

- **Categories**. Categories represent available *choices* or *varieties*. They should be exhaustive and mutually exclusive. These are generally finite in number, where the range of options associated with the attribute is defined. New choices or varieties can be added to the categories available, as long as they don't overlap with existing categories.

The values of some categories are *ordinal*: they follow an expected order. The days of the week are an example of a category where the values have an order: one can compare if a day is before or after another.

- **Quantities**. Quantities are *discrete* (countable) numbers, *continuous* (variable) numbers or a quantitative *range* (an interval). Quantitates also encompass time values including dates, and geospatial values such as longitude and latitude.

- **Names and Verbal Descriptions**. Names and other verbal descriptions can have unlimited variations. A thing or concept can be given a unique name, or can be described with words in various ways. Some real world entities have both official and widely-used alternative names.

Biographic information about a person illustrates the different kinds of values:

- The person's name may be unique.

- Their place of birth may be a category value, provided the categories listed for geographic locations are sufficiently large and exhaustive.

- Their profession will also be a category value, as will their nationality (they may have more than one of each of these values, however).

- Their age is a quantitative value, based on their date of birth.

- A description of their career may involve verbal description, together with a table contains dates (quantities) and awards (categories.)

Alternate names for Values

Technical people may refer to values using other terms, depending on their priorities.

Identifiers

Identifiers is sometimes used for name values

Terms

Terms is sometimes used for category values

Data

When used to refer to values, *data* is generally used for category values and quantities, but not for verbal descriptions.

[22] This list is representative, and by no means complete.
[23] This paragraph could, in principle, be reused and be managed as a content *component*. It is possible to manage with metadata more granular units of content such as snippets or text variables. For the purposes of our discussion of content items, we are focusing on the management of independent items of content rather than context-dependent ones.
[24] Donald Chestnut and Kevin Nichols, *UX For Dummies*, p. 132
[25] Entities are generally *tangible things*, or *intangible services* such as airline flights with defined beginnings and ends. But not always. *Well-understood concepts* such as Love or Democracy (the kind that have entries on Wikipedia) can be entities as well, though they can be trickier to identify in metadata.
[26] Compared to noun-based entities, entities representing actions often follow more formal criteria. The kinds of actions that qualify as entities will be governed by a specific metadata standard that defines what action-based entities represent. An example of a scenario where actions might be useful to represent as entities is illustrated in the social music platform example in the previous chapter.
[27] When used as a content type, a topic conveys the structure of the content and its purpose, but not the specific subject of the content or the entities it addresses. Indicating the purpose of content is not the same as indicating "what each topic is about." See, for example, Erik Hennum et al, "Subject Classification with DITA and SKOS", *IBM developerWorks*, October 18, 2005, `http://www.ibm.com/developerworks/xml/library/x-dita10/`
[28] This example is intentionally simplified to keep the focus on entities and entity types. In practice, one would likely want to identify more specifically the kind of iPhone, which would involve a model number and perhaps a model variant. The issue of product architecture is discussed in greater detail in `Chapter 8`.

Chapter 4. Metadata Applied: Use Cases Across the Content Lifecycle

CHAPTER PREVIEW

Metadata makes content easier to work with in numerous ways. Publishers can use metadata at different phases of the lifecycle of content. Metadata is useful during **content creation** (helping with locating content and workflow), **content delivery** (supporting customization and personalization in content), and **content assessment and prioritization** (assisting the tracking and management of content that's been published). In addition to being useful to employees within your own organization, web content metadata is useful to external parties and platforms, including search engines such as Google, social media platforms such as Facebook, content aggregation platforms and software such as iTunes, and specifications designed to support the exchange of content called Application Programming Interfaces (APIs).

Metadata Makes Content Publication More Manageable

Metadata is useful to many different kinds of people, so little surprise that it plays a key role throughout the entire content lifecycle. Metadata supports key processes in the content lifecycle: content creation, content delivery, content management, and content assessment and prioritization. In additional to supporting internal processes, metadata facilitates the delivery of content to external parties in a wide range of ways. (See Figure 4.1.)

Figure 4.1

Content Across the Lifecycle

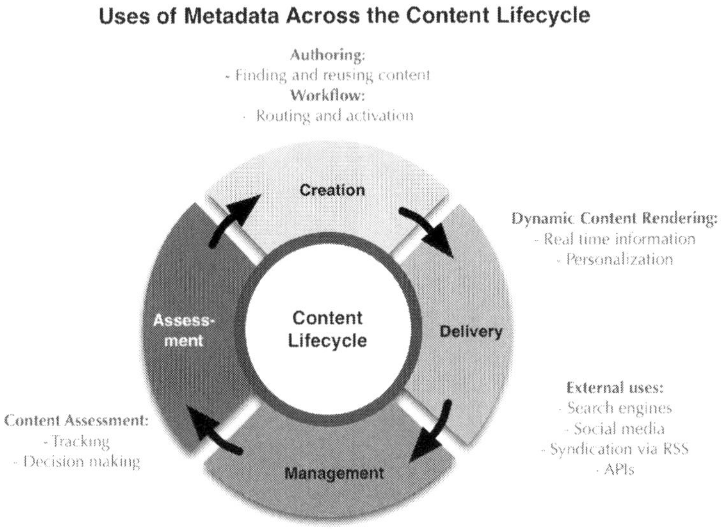

Uses of Metadata Across the Content Lifecycle

Authoring:
- Finding and reusing content

Workflow:
- Routing and activation

Dynamic Content Rendering:
- Real time information
- Personalization

External uses:
- Search engines
- Social media
- Syndication via RSS
- APIs

Content Assessment:
- Tracking
- Decision making

Creation · Delivery · Management · Assessment

Content Lifecycle

How Publishers Use Metadata Internally

Metadata serves as a key enabler and bridge integrating different processes within an organization. It integrates different resources in an organization's content infrastructure, such as its content management system, digital asset management system, analytics engine, and customer relationship management system.

Let's look at how metadata facilitates the publication of content at different stages by supporting different tasks.

Phase: Content Creation.

1. Authoring

Authoring involves all aspects of content creation, including writing, editing and approvals, or the production and post-production of media. Metadata improves the efficiency of operations, and the productivity of content assets. What's been called *editorial metadata* is metadata specifically intended to help authors and editors manage their tasks more effectively. For example, a content management system might display metadata indicating that a content item "needs review."[29]

2. Finding and Reusing Content Assets

One of the most important benefits of metadata is that it lets authors know what content already exists on a topic. Suppose you wanted to use a photo of your facility in Ireland. You can locate that photo using by searching for photos matching the metadata description. Many different content assets are frequently reused: graphics, branding collateral, and legal disclaimers. Metadata identifies these, and indicates how they should be used.

Reusing existing content provides two big benefits: it saves time, and it reduces content duplication.

3. Workflow

Administrative metadata supports various workflow actions, helping to reduce the effort for authors and approvers. Metadata indicates the status of content in a workflow, and can be used to automatically publish or take down content according to predefined criteria such as dates.

Phase: Content Delivery

1. Dynamic Content Rendering

Metadata allows content to adapt to current circumstances, and to be tailored to the needs of an individual. Metadata can work with business rules to select what content to display in given circumstances.[30] For example, if a publisher wanted to offer some of their content to be available on a smartwatch, they would indicate with metadata which fields to display on such devices.

2. Enabling Real-Time Information

Metadata supports the inclusion in content of real-time information delivered through feeds or via user queries to support data-driven documents and apps. It allows the most current information to be included within the body of a text, or within a table, map, chart or graphics.

3. Supporting Personalization

Metadata is vital to supporting content personalization. For example, it can be used to provide location specific content based on a user's current geo-location. The metadata could indicate *location variants* of the content, so that only the relevant variant is delivered.

Metadata can also support personalization that tailors the content displayed based on user behaviors, such as the success a student achieved in an e-learning quiz.

Phases: Content Management, Content Assessment / Prioritization.

1. Content Analysis

Content publishers are concerned about the impact of their content and seek to measure the performance of content in greater detail. Metadata plays a growing role linking content performance to organizational performance, identifying which *themes*, *formats* and *messages* deliver greatest value to the organization.[31]

2. Updating and Retiring Content

Metadata can indicate when it is time to review content to see if it needs updating or retirement. Content can have a flag indicating how far in the future it should be reviewed to see if changes are needed. An important role of metadata is *versioning*, so that authors and content managers can track changes to content over time.

3. Tracking and Decision Making

Analytics programs can track user behaviors using tools called *tag managers*.[32] Analysts can identify trends in use of content according to topic, optimize content on specific topics using A/B testing, and discover if content coverage needs rebalancing.

---

[29] The concept of editorial metadata and the example cited are taken from Deane Barker's book, *Web Content Management Systems*.

[30] The mechanism that allows specific elements of content (expressed as metadata attributes) to work with business rules is called a content model. An example of a content model is presented in `Chapter` 5. Content models are a topic worthy of a book-length treatment. A good introduction is by Rachel Lovinger, "Content Modeling: A Master Skill" *A List Apart*, April 24, 2012, `http://alistapart.com/article/content-modelling-a-master-skill`

[31] The data used to do content analysis is known as *content analytics*. Content analytics is a field of measurement that overlaps with *web analytics* but is distinct from it. Where web analytics often focuses page-level tactical and technical issues such as click through rates, bounce rates and page redirects, content analytics may focus on higher level issues such as content engagement by topic, or long term audience loyalty.

[32] In another example of how the same term can have different meanings, here tags refer to computer code rather than to metadata. Tag management coordinates the use of Javascript

"tags" to track user events relating to content. While the Javascript tags themselves aren't metadata, they can work in conjunction with metadata to help analytics professionals get a deeper understanding of how content is performing. An example of how this works is explained in "Tracking Semantic SEO with Google Analytics and Tealium", `https://www.analyticspros.com/blog/tag-management/tracking-semantic-seo-with-google-analytics/` Such analytics tracking of metadata detail is not yet common, but should become so in the future.

How External Distribution Channels Use Metadata

Metadata is essential to enabling outside parties to obtain your content in a format that is useful to them. Different kinds of consumers of content require different formats, so it is important that metadata is available to support the full range of needs. We'll show what formats each require, and will later explain what these formats involve.

Search Engines

Search engines are one of the most important consumers of metadata. Search engines come in many guises. While **Google** is the best-known search engine, other search platforms make extensive use of metadata. These include shopping aggregators such as **Amazon** and **e-Bay**, bookings aggregators such as **travel** and **concert booking** sites, and enterprise search engines that index product specifications and product support information.

How Search Engines Use Metadata

Search engines such as Google and Bing use metadata to identity what content is about. Traditionally, they have largely relied on key words or phrases used in the text of an article to determine the topic of the content. But using key words are not very precise: they can be ambiguous, and the meaning associated with the key words can't easily be extracted for other uses. As a result, search engines increasingly rely on semantic metadata that indicates the precise entities mentioned in content.

Exactly how search engines use metadata is subject to much speculation and controversy, since search engines perform exceedingly complex operations evaluating content, and they don't reveal precisely how they weight different factors. But patents from search engines provide some clues into factors that they consider, and these factors can involve metadata. This diagram in `Figure 4.2`, from a Microsoft patent titled "Using Categorical Metadata to Rank Search Results", provides an example of how metadata is used to index both content and search queries to produce search results.[33] While the specific details in the diagram aren't important to understand, what's important to know that search engines use metadata, and that providing it will make it easier for search engines to understand the meaning of your content.

Figure 4.2

Microsoft Patent for "Using Categorical Metadata to Rank Search Results"

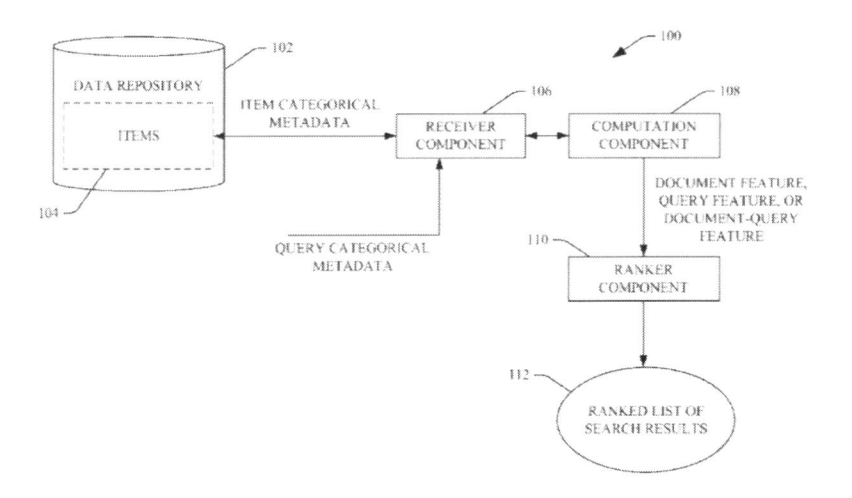

Types of Metadata Used by Search Engines

Search engines use a wide range of metadata to evaluate web content, such as an article's page title, and the titles of hyperlinks within an article. Search Engine Optimization is a specialized field devoted to understanding and optimizing all the elements within content that can affect search discovery. Search engines pay attention to two critical metadata dimensions: the Meta description, and schema.org markup, both of which are used when displaying search results.[34]

HTML Meta Description. This is a short description (around 150 characters) added to an item of content explaining what it is. The description may appear in search engine results below the title. It is an important signal to audiences what the content is about.

This example from Google illustrates the meta description.[35]

```
<!DOCTYPE html> <html>   <head>
<meta charset="utf-8">
<meta name="Description" CONTENT="Author: A.N.
Author, Illustrator: P. Picture, Category:
Books, Price:  £9.24, Length: 784 pages"> ❶
<meta name="google-site-verification"
content="+nxGUD...34="/>
<title>Example Books - high-quality used books
for children</title>
<meta name="robots"
content="noindex,nofollow">
```

❶ The Meta element with a Description. The description value associated with the CONTENT attribute.

Google notes: "In some situations this description is used as a part of the snippet shown in the search results."[36]

Schema.org Markup. A family of markup known as schema.org is used to enable what's become known as semantic search. Schema.org has emerged as one of the most important kinds of metadata, largely due to search engine's reliance on it. What it can do and how it works will be discussed in detail in `Chapter 7`.

Social Media

Social media includes consumer applications such as Facebook as well as business-focused applications intended to coordinate team interactions. Social media metadata can describe a rich set of interactions between people, topics, and activities. Some social media metadata is proprietary and not visible or accessible to publishers or users. Where social media platforms rely on interactions with parties and content outside of their platforms, they use public metadata to facilitate these interactions.

How Social Media Platforms Use Metadata

Social media has become one of the most important channels for distributing and discovering content. Unlike search engines, where users explicitly indicate the kind of content they want, social media relies on a combination of social affiliations and user behaviors to stream content to users based on their implicit wants. Content metadata helps to match content that might be of interest to people.

Different social platforms use different metadata standards. Twitter, for example, uses a format called Twitter cards. Among U.S.-based social media channels, **Open Graph** has emerged as a widely used standard, and some non-English social networks seem to be adopting it as well.

The Open Graph protocol provides a simple description of content. Open Graph metadata allows interaction with content to become associated with the social profile of an individual in a social network. Developed by **Facebook**, Open Graph is also used by **LinkedIn**, **Google Plus** and **Pinterest**, among others. How it is used will be discussed in Chapter 7.

Syndication: RSS & Atom

Really Simple Syndication (**RSS**) is format used to distribute a content feed, typically newsfeeds, blog posts or podcasts to subscribers.[37] Content aggregators such as iTunes use RSS to package delivery of content to their subscribers.

RSS uses a markup called **XML** to indicate basic information about the content, such as title, date, creator and source link to the article, audio file or video. Additional metadata can include information about the length of the item, the category the content relates to, and a profile image to represent the content.

Atom is a similar, alternative format to RSS.[38]

Content as a Service: APIs

An **Application Programming Interface** (API) is specification for how content is made available. The publisher commits to making certain content available in certain machine-friendly formats that can be used by other parties, in exchange for other parties agreeing to conditions the publisher specifies.

Web APIs are used to make one's content available to different websites and apps, and also to incorporate content from other platforms into one's own content. For example, Google makes **Google Maps** available as an API, so that other parties can incorporate Google Map content within their own content. The **New York Times** offers an API for its list of best selling books. It is common for publishers to be both producers and consumers of APIs. In addition to offering a range of APIs, the New York Times uses APIs from other publishers.

Content management systems (CMS) often include API functionality. Publishers can use their CMS to distribute their web content to other parties via an API.

APIs can be either public or private. With a public API, content is available to everyone who follows the terms of use, while private APIs generally involve a legal contract with a large customer, perhaps a business partner. Some APIs are developed for internal use within an organization, so that content can be used in different ways in different applications.

API Format

Parties can access content programmatically using one of the key HTTP (HyperText Transfer Protocol) verbs:

- GET (*retrieve and show content*)

- POST (*add or insert content*)

- PUT (*update content*)

- DELETE (*remove content*).

GET is the most commonly used in web content publishing. GET statements request and retrieve content that is returned wrapped within a metadata description.[39]

An example from the Associated Press will illustrates how an API works. The following API query will retrieve photos that have metadata indicating the person in the photo as being both Tom Cruise and Katie Holmes.[40]

```
GET
https://api.ap.org/v2/search?apiKey={apiKey}&p
erson=Tom+Cruise&person=Katie+Holmes
```

The Associated Press API provides the ability to retrieve images and articles based on various metadata *parameters* such as location, event, subject and creation date.

Most APIs require a unique *API key* (an ID code that identifies the receiving party), which would be included within the brackets in the example to gain access permission.

Metadata Used in APIs

The metadata enclosing the content allows it to be mutually intelligible to both the requesting and supplying parties. APIs generally aim to be *self-describing* so that developers can understand what the metadata refers to. However, some degree of documentation is normally required to explain the package to others. Sometimes hundreds of separate metadata fields are available, and developers need to understand the distinctions between them.

A format called **JSON** is the most common metadata format used in APIs. We'll discuss JSON in Chapter 6 on data exchange standards.

---

[33] Microsoft Corporation, "Using categorical metadata to rank search results", US Patent 9,020,936 B2, Date of Patent: April 28, 2015, available at `http://patft.uspto.gov/netahtml/PTO/srchnum.htm`

[34] I will leave the discussion of what role, if any, metadata plays in the *ranking* of search results to those who are professional SEO specialists. Metadata's importance to search engines does not depend on whether it influences search rankings, since it influences the visibility of content more broadly. Metadata delivers value by increasing the likelihood that audiences will notice information relating to the content, and will utilize the content to support their goals.

[35] "Meta tags that Google understands", `https://support.google.com/webmasters/answer/79812?hl=en`

[36] *ibid.*

[37] "RSS 2.0 Specification", `https://validator.w3.org/feed/docs/rss2.html`

[38] The Internet Society, "The Atom Syndication Format", RFC 4287, `https://tools.ietf.org/html/rfc4287`

[39] Although APIs are most often used in web content to get metadata, they can also be used to submit metadata, and can even combine the submission and retrieval of metadata. An

interesting example comes from a "Recipe Analysis API" by Edaman. Publishers can use this API to submit metadata relating to food recipes (the ingredients used in dishes and their quantities), and the API will return metadata providing the nutritional value and dietary characteristics of the dish. See Documentation at https://developer.edamam.com/edamam-docs-nutrition-api

[40] Associated Press, "AP CONTENT API 2.9 Developer's Guide", p.10, https://developer.ap.org/sites/default/files/AP_Content_API_Developer_Guide.pdf

Chapter 5. Metadata Functions

Chapter Preview

Different kinds of metadata serve different functions.

Administrative metadata tracks the history of content items, such as when items were last updated, and by whom. It can also provide status information about content that is being revised, or about published content that needs to be taken down.

Descriptive metadata specifies the subject of the content, which might be a topic tag, an abstract, or a semantic markup noting entities in the content.

Structural metadata indicates how components of content should be used within content items. The HTML `<section>` element is an example of structural metadata.

Rights metadata encompasses metadata that defines copyright, permissions and obligations, as well as indicating credit for the content. The most widely known example of rights metadata is the Creative Commons framework, but other frameworks are important as well, especially in the area of photographic images.

Technical metadata indicates the technical characteristics of files, such as their format and size. Technical metadata is especially important in rich media such as videos.

The different kinds of metadata work together to provide a comprehensive description of content items. We can understand the specific metadata attributes that should be captured by looking at some everyday content types we encounter online: articles, YouTube videos, and Podcasts.

Content requirements should also consider how web content metadata needs to be coordinated with business data managed in transactional IT systems.

Metadata Functions and Purposes

What dimensions of content are important to address with metadata? What kinds of questions about web content can metadata answer? Different kinds of metadata exist to support different kinds of requirements. To develop comprehensive metadata requirements for web content, and ensure that the entire content lifecycle is managed appropriately, publishers need to account for the different functions and purposes metadata can address.

Metadata is grouped according to the different functions and purposes it serves. These functions are:

- Administrative
- Descriptive
- Structural
- Rights and permissions
- Technical.

These different functions work together to provide a comprehensive profile of the content. (See Figure 5.1.)

Figure 5.1
Functions of Metadata

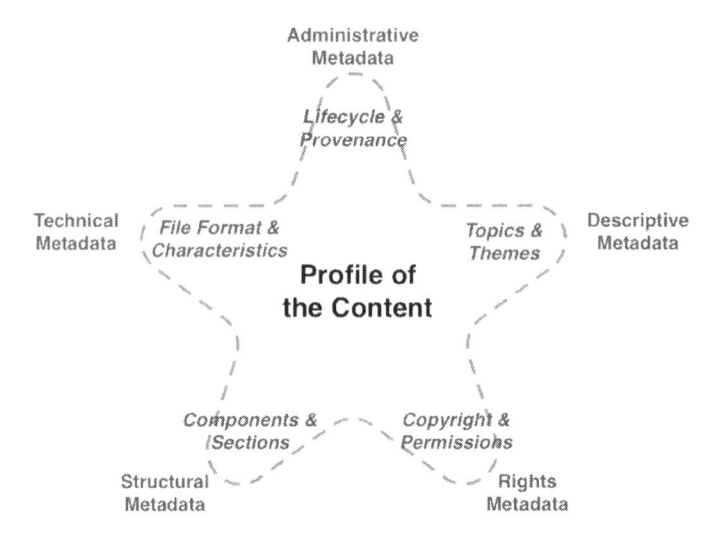

```
                    Administrative
                      Metadata
                   Lifecycle &
                   Provenance

Technical      File Format &         Topics &        Descriptive
Metadata       Characteristics       Themes          Metadata
                         Profile of
                         the Content

               Components &      Copyright &
               Sections          Permissions
              Structural                      Rights
              Metadata                        Metadata
```

Administrative Metadata

Administrative metadata provides a record about the content. It answers: "What *specific instance* is this item?" It is especially important when there may be different *versions* of the same basic content: different *revisions*, or *languages*. When *multiple formats* exist for a content item, for example an interview that has both an audio file and a transcript, administrative metadata can track these relationships. In combination with Rights metadata, it also indicates the intellectual property profile of the item.

Administrative metadata is often not visible to audiences, so it may be less familiar than other kinds of metadata. Administrative metadata can indicate the provenance and lifecycle characteristics of the content.

- **Provenance Data.** Provenance data indicates author or creator, and source (if content acquired from an external party). Internal provenance data might include approvers, reviewers, or persons making updates.

- **Lifecycle Data.** Lifecycle data includes retrospective and prospective information about dates: date created, revised, archived (retrospective), or date to be published or date to be withdrawn (prospective). It includes associated status information for content such as draft, approved, pending publication, published, or withdrawn.

Administrative Metadata in a Content Model

This content model for articles from the U.S. Government indicates some kinds of administrative metadata (shown with arrows). Only some of these fields will be visible to audiences.

Article Content Model for US Government Websites
- Title (Required, Only one allowed)
  - ShortTitle (Optional, Only one allowed)
  - FullTitle (Required, Only one allowed)
- Description (Required, Only one allowed)
  - ShortDescription (Optional, Only one allowed)
  - DetailedDescription (Required, Only one allowed)
- URL (Optional, Only one allowed)
- → **ArticleType** (Optional, Only one allowed)
- → **Dates** (Optional, Only one allowed)
  - → **DatePosted** (Required, Only one allowed)
  - → **DateFirstPublished** (Optional, Only one allowed)
  - → **DateLastModified** (Optional, Only one allowed)
  - → **DateReleased** (Optional, Only one allowed)
- → **SourceOrganization** (Required, Only one allowed)
- → **Contributor** (Optional, Only one allowed)
- → **Author** (Optional, Multiple allowed)
- → **InLanguage** (Optional, Only one allowed)
- → **Audience** (Optional, Multiple allowed)
- References (Optional, Multiple allowed)
- Topics (Required, Multiple allowed)
- ArticleBody (Required, Only one allowed)
  - ArticleSection (Required, Multiple allowed)
    - SectionTitle (Required, Only one allowed)
    - SectionBody (Required, Only one allowed)
- → **RelatedMultimedia** (Optional, Only one allowed)
  - → **Video** (Optional, Multiple allowed)
  - → **Audio** (Optional, Multiple allowed)
  - → **Image** (Optional, Multiple allowed)
- → **AggregateRating** (Optional, Only one allowed)
- → **IsBasedOnURL** (Optional, Multiple allowed)
- → **RelatedURLs** (Optional, Multiple allowed)

Source: U.S. General Services Administration.[41]

This content model illustrates the wide range of information addressed by administrative metadata. It includes related content, target audience segments, user ratings of content, and fine distinctions concerning the content's source, authorship, and contributors.

What Administrative Metadata does

Administrative metadata can act like the data captured by a fitness or life tracking app. In the background, it monitors what's happening. It also provides direction to authors and computers about actions to take.

1. Records the Content's History

Administrative metadata is often auto-generated by content systems based on actions relating to the content. It provides a history of the content: who created it, when it was created, and subsequent activity. Some of this metadata, for example author and data of publication, is published and viewable by audiences. Other administrative metadata such as information on status or approvers may be only used and viewed internally.

2. Supports Internationalization and Localization

Metadata can indicate different versions of content intended for different global audiences. In HTML, the `lang` tag is used to declare what language a content item is, and one can even indicate within articles when words are from different languages.[42] Browsers, spellcheckers and other tools rely on these tags to interpret content appropriately.

Metadata can also help translators localize content. The **Internationalization Tag Set** enables content to be marked up with notes relating to the translation and localization of text.[43]

The W3C notes: "The usefulness of language tagging has increased over recent years, as technology has progressed, and it will continue to increase as we go forward."[44]

Applications of Administrative Metadata

Administrative metadata supports content workflows. It can support *workflow automation* such as routing content to appropriate reviewers, and scheduling of publication and removal of content. Administrative metadata can also support how content systems prioritize the delivery of content. For example, program rules can use metadata about the age of the content to rank where it will show up in internal search results.

Administrative Metadata and Content Analytics

Administrative metadata generally refers to actions and activity taken by the publisher of content. A more expansive view of administrative metadata would consider log data relating to how content is viewed or used as also qualifying, especially if any decisions are made automatically on the basis of how much the content is used. Content analytics can play a prominent role in the lifecycle of a content item, and it can be beneficial to think about such information as part of the administrative metadata relating to the item. The recorded activity of any actor or agent upon the content that has business consequences contributes to the profile of the content's history.

Jeffrey Pomerantz, an information scientist and scholar of metadata, refers to analytics about the use of content as "use metadata", though he notes that term has not been widely adopted.[45]

Descriptive Metadata

Descriptive metadata helps people find what they want, and enhances the relevance of content. Semantic metadata is a form of descriptive metadata, where the description follows a formal, commonly agreed schema that indicates the meaning and relationships of metadata.[46]

Descriptive metadata is important to all phases of the content lifecycle. It helps authors locate content to revise and reuse, it helps audiences access content, and it is an important parameter to track in content analytics.

Examples of descriptive metadata include:

- Title
- Abstract
- Index terms
- Categories used in menu systems

- Subject tags

- Semantic markup indicating entities in content

What Descriptive Metadata Does

Fundamentally, descriptive metadata answers: "What is this content about?" Descriptive metadata can be applied to content items, and to entities referred to within content items.

1. **Provides General Content Description.**

    Metadata can describe content items using general descriptions that indicate the subject or purpose of a piece of content audiences will consume. The description can take many forms, such as a narrative description (such as a short abstract) or category labels. Descriptive metadata can be used to describe collections of content items as well. For example, it can indicate all articles relating to a general topic.

2. **Describes Specific Occurrences.**

    Detailed descriptions can identify specific entities mentioned in the body of content, such as the names of people or companies. They are especially useful when the entities mentioned are not the main subject identified by the general content description.

Applications of Descriptive Metadata

The most important role of descriptive metadata is in enhancing content discovery. Descriptive metadata helps audiences locate and browse content. A major application is search engines, both multi-site search engines such as Google and vertical search engines such as Amazon or Travelocity. The other major application is supporting site functionality, such as:

- Faceted browsing
- The generation of data-driven content
- The presentation of related links
- Sorting and filtering of lists
- Displaying behavioral data related to audience engagement with topics.[47]

Structural Metadata

Structural metadata expresses overall content structure. It reflects how authors have organized elements in the content. It indicates to information architects what content is available when defining user interface elements such as boxes or widgets. These user interface elements are implemented as content templates, which utilize structural metadata.

Structural metadata provides a skeleton for content as it is delivered to audiences. It defines how compound content items fit together.

Structural metadata describes specific content chunks or content components that may:

1. Need to be seen separately from the content with which it is associated, or

2. Be used in multiple contexts.

It can identify components such as:

- Narrative section
- A sidebar
- A pull-quote
- Video segment
- Photo
- Map.

What Structural Metadata does

Structural metadata plays several important roles.

1. **Defines Distinct Components within Content Objects.**

   Structural metadata within an item of content is similar to well-defined labels and headings that are used consistently in content to indicate the organizational pattern of the content. HTML markup provides basic structural elements such as the `<title>`, `<body>`, and `<table>`. In HTML5 markup, structural metadata includes sectioning content such as `<article>`, `<aside>`, `<nav>`, and `<section>`.

Publishers can define more specific structure within elements if needed by using attributes. Some front-end developers refer to these structural elements as "semantic HTML" to distinguish elements that have a structural role from elements that only effect presentation.

2. **Organizes Content Components and Their Relationships**.

Structural elements are related to each other when they are presented together to audiences — they belong to a common content type, the overall structure of a content item. All content items belonging to the same content type will have the same overall structure. For example, an article might always include a title, but a photo might not.

3. **Enables Reuse of Content Components**.

Structure allows components of content to be reused and recombined in different contexts. For example, a specific table may be included within an article, or as sidebar. By identifying the role of the content, structural metadata makes the content modular.

4. **Is Represented in a Content Model of Elements Used Across Different Content Types**.

Structural metadata defines different content types, indicating which generic elements always appear together, such as in blog post or an event announcement. Different content types are related to one another when they share elements. For example, one content type might be a more detailed version of another, such as when a long version of the event announcement includes a map, while the short version doesn't. The mapping of structures used by different content types is represented in a content model.

Application of Structural Metadata

Structural metadata performs several functions. For audiences, it provides a point of access into a body of content, enabling navigation. Access may be visual, such as providing labels and headings for chunks of content that audiences can scan and notice. The access can also be interactive, providing hyperlinks and filters to reach content of interest.

For publishers, structural metadata helps to define units of content that can be reused in different contexts.

Assembly of Objects by a CMS into Rendered Content Viewed by Audience. Structural metadata is important in content management. It defines the building blocks of different views of content. Content management systems grab structural elements to deliver content dynamically according to defined rules.

Rights and Permissions Metadata

Rights metadata helps prevent content misuse. If ignored, legal issues can ensue. Some forms of content, such as music and photos, can have multiple layers of copyright associated with them.

A well-known example of rights metadata is Creative Commons, which will be discussed shortly. There are other important frameworks that are less familiar to most people. Before we look at details of creative commons and other frameworks, we need to understand more about what this kind of metadata does.

What Rights and Permissions Metadata does

Rights metadata addresses two aspects: content permissions and content credits. Publishers use permissions metadata to assert ownership of content, or indicate how they understand the ownership of the content. Publishers also have duties relating to content. One duty is indicating proper credit to creators of content.

Teams involved with metadata requirements need to consider copyright and other legal issues for several reasons:

- Web content routinely reuses existing content, so it's important to be able to identify **who owns that content**

- Because of the vast volumes of content that must be managed, publishers increasingly rely on the ability of machines to discover **contractual information**

- There are efforts to try to **standardize contracts** relating to content usage, and standardize how these standard clauses are presented within machine-readable metadata.

Content Permissions

Content permissions typically relates to copyright, but also might include information relating to an *embargo*.

Copyright is a complex topic, but an unavoidable one.[48] The discussion that follows is not designed to offer expert legal advice on copyright, but to alert you to how copyright and metadata can intersect.

Broadly speaking, copyright can fall into four categories:

- Copyright owned by the publisher
- Copyright owned by a third party

- Copyright that's in the public domain (*for older works*)

- Copyright that has orphan status (*for older works*).[49]

The status of third party works can be involved. For some visual works, more than one party can have a copyright – for example, both the creator and owner hold specific rights.[50] Even content that has been assigned a creative commons license still entails conditions, unless the creator has opted for a "no rights reserved" declaration.

When rights and permissions metadata is missing, the issue of who owns the copyright can become confused. From a legal perspective, in the United States at least, one does not necessarily need to explicitly claim copyright, through registration with the copyright office, to enjoy copyright protection for original creative works that one has authored. But when there is no explicit trail concerning copyright status, the likelihood that copyrighted material will be used without permission increases. That becomes a headache whether you are the creator who has had your content taken, or whether you are a publisher who is using someone else's content without being aware that it is under copyright.

The use of content created by others, or the provision of one's own content for others can use, will commonly involve some kind of license that determines the conditions of use. Rights confer *permissions*, such as how the content can be used (such as display or play only, in contrast with permissions that let users download an item of content). Permissions entail *duties*—issues such as payments or when content must be deleted. They may also entail *restrictions*, such as:

- **Geographies** or regions where content is permitted use

- **Time period** when content may be used

- **Distribution channels** in which content may be distributed.

Content licensing has become a big industry. A growing range of firms are creating content available for others to use through license, and many online publishers are choosing to incorporate licensed content as part of the content they deliver to their audiences.[51] The terms and conditions of content licenses, including statements of content ownership, rights granted, and restrictions imposed, are starting to be specified in formal metadata frameworks that are machine-readable.

Content Credits

We can see the need for content to be properly attributed in many everyday situations where we wonder who was responsible for some content nugget. We come across a wise-sounding quotation, and see it ascribed to various famous people, from ancient Greek philosophers to retired sports coaches. Or we see an amazing image on social media and wonder where it came from. Perhaps someone found it online somewhere, uploaded the image to their social media channel, which was shared widely. Due to its popularity the image gets republished online again in various articles discussing the image. Both these examples illustrate the problems arising when content credits are not available in metadata.[52]

When creating content for publication, one will often want to indicate who the creator is in content credits. In many cases the credit is simple: presenting an attribute called "creator" and providing the name of person responsible. In other cases, more than one person can be involved. News agencies that offer photos may provide credits indicating the photographer, the caption writer, and sometimes the "credit"— the name of the person who provided the image to the news agency.[53]

For externally sourced content, credit must be explicitly acknowledged. Organizations that provide content through APIs such a Reuters and Yahoo have *attribution guidelines* that indicate how the content must be presented.[54] Yahoo, for example, requires a link to Yahoo's website, as well as using a use of a logo stating "Powered by Yahoo!".[55]

Even if the content is public domain (for example, a historic image), it is good form to acknowledge who created the work, and when it was created, if these are known.

Specific Rights and Permissions Metadata Frameworks

Different options are available to express rights and permissions, depending on the kind of content, and the kinds of rights involved. Two broad frameworks are available: one oriented to public information, and one geared to the contractual needs of commercial publishers. The general term used for metadata frameworks covering rights and permissions is *Rights Expression Languages (REL)*.[56]

Content that is licensed for public use is generally described using the Creative Commons Rights Expression Language (CC REL), or its companion for data, the Open Data Commons.

Creative Commons. Creative commons is license framework to indicate how people can use content. It is currently divided into six tiers, that range from allowing others to redistribute content non-commercially with proper attribution, to allowing others to change the content (develop *derivative content*) and use it for profit provided attribution is given. All creative commons content is freely distributed, but it can impose restrictions on what users can do with the content.

Restrictions relate to the intent of use (prohibition of noncommercial uses and prohibition of derivative use). Duties can relate to how derivative content is licensed (*share alike*, where "adapted material [are made] available under the same terms and conditions").[57]

The six levels of Creative Commons licenses represent different combinations of features:

1. BY (*attribution only*)

2. BY-SA (*attribution and share alike*)

3. BY-NC (*attribution and noncommercial use*)

4. BY-NC-SA (*attribution, noncommercial use and share alike*)

5. BY-ND (*attribution and no derivatives*)

6. BY-NC-ND (*attribution, noncommercial use and no derivatives*).[58]

The following example of Creative Commons metadata will show how it operates.[59] A the license for a photo is being specified in metadata. The ID of the photo is this example is a uniform resource name (URN).[60] It is licensed under the basic attribution license, under the terms of version 3.0 of the license.

```
<p>The document example.pdf is licensed under
a <a about="urn:sha1:MSMBC5...ZHCY2MD"
rel="license"
href="http://creativecommons.org/license/by/3.
0/"> Creative Commons Attribution 3.0</a>
license.  ❶    </a> </p>
```

❶ A machine readable statement about the licensing is provided by the link to the Creative Commons website. A computer crawling this content will know the exact terms

101

of the content permission based on the specific URL link that is included in the metadata.

Most users of Creative Commons metadata use an code similar the example above. Creative Commons does provide a more detailed framework that can be used to specify permissions in more granular detail.[61] Figure 5.2 illustrates the overall framework, where copyright for works can involve specific permissions, requirements and prohibitions.[62]

Figure 5.2

Creative Commons Schema Framework

Creative Commons Metadata Framework

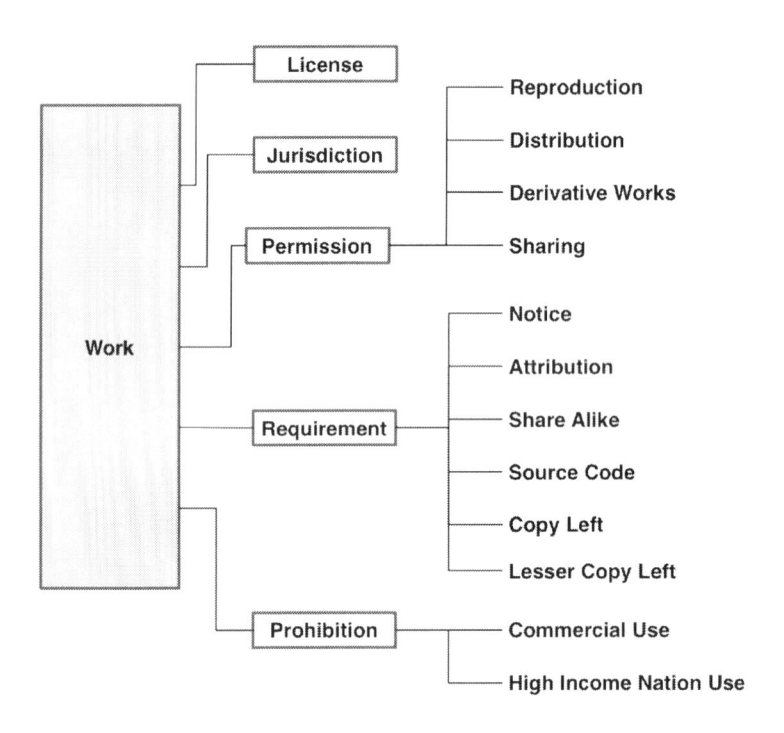

Work
- License
- Jurisdiction
- Permission
  - Reproduction
  - Distribution
  - Derivative Works
  - Sharing
- Requirement
  - Notice
  - Attribution
  - Share Alike
  - Source Code
  - Copy Left
  - Lesser Copy Left
- Prohibition
  - Commercial Use
  - High Income Nation Use

Open Data Commons. The Open Data Commons is similar to Creative Commons in intent, but oriented toward the needs of data sets. It puts data in the public domain. Much content such as maps is generated from databases. Other content will recombine data from multiple sources. The rights to using the underlying data become important.

Open Data Commons is based on three kinds of licenses:

1. Public Domain Dedication and License (PDDL)
2. Attribution License (ODC-By)
3. Open Database License (ODbL).[63]

Commercial rights frameworks fall under the general area of *digital rights management* (DRM). DRM includes rights metadata, but is much broader, covering technologies such as watermarking and digital forensics.

Several metadata frameworks for commercial rights management exist. Two frameworks to be familiar with are the Open Digital Rights Language (ODRL) and IPTC's Photo Rights (RightsML).

Open Digital Rights Language (ODRL). ODRL is a long-established voluntary standard for specifying rights and permissions in metadata. The full specification can be complex. While not many publishers use ODRL directly, ODRL has indirect influence on other metadata standards and implementations publishers are likely to use. ODRL can be used to specify many dimensions of contracts relating to the licensing of content.[64] It is similar to Creative Commons in having permissions, prohibitions and duties (called requirements in CC REL), but it also offers a rich set of terms covering actions relating to content use, and parties such as assigner and assignee. These terms can be used to construct an offer for the use of a content asset, which can specify payment necessary to use the content, subject to conditions made in the offer.

ODRL is capable of expressing a wide range of rights and permissions, even indicating whether a party has the right to use text-to-speech functionality with content.

IPTC Photo Rights (RightsML). The International Press Telecommunications Council (IPTC) developed a metadata standard called the Rights Expression Language (RightsML) for images and other media.[65] The IPTC explains the benefits of RightsML as follows: "'With RightsML, every single piece of content distributed by a publisher can be annotated with machine-readable instructions that spell out the particular permissions and restrictions for a piece of content. For example 'this photo can be used in print but not in broadcast' or 'this photo can be used online for 30 days after it was created but print use requires additional licenses.'"[66]

RightsML is based on ODRL. It is widely used by organizations that license content to others such as Reuters and Getty Images. While RightsML is largely used for photos, it can be applied to other media such as videos.

Applications of Rights and Permissions Metadata

Some rights metadata is made visible to readers, so that they understand who owns content and how the content can be used. Rights metadata can also be used in the context of automated content management.

Workflow and Compliance. Rights metadata is used internally to support workflow, and used externally to assure legal compliance .

There can be much variation in the rights profiles of different content being sourced and published, making management complex. RightsML includes machine-readable instructions to support automation of discovery and management tasks.

Generation of Natural Language Contracts. The IPTC has been developing software that can translate the rights metadata into natural language automatically. The ability of computer programs to generate natural language statements based on machine-readable metadata can reduce the effort needed to write human readable statements that can involve many variations.

Technical Metadata

Technical metadata is probably the kind of metadata of least immediate interest to audiences, but it is vitally important to the proper functioning of content. The details embedded in technical metadata either allows the content to perform seamlessly, or it can ruin the user experience, such as when a person can't view a video because the video file is not compatible with their device.

Technical metadata examples include:

- Video file format and characteristics
- Photo format size and resolution
- eBook format
- Time code information for video and audio files.

A single delivery channel may involve various formats. For example, a podcast indicates attachment of a media type, which could be MP3 (audio), M4A (audio), MP4 (video), M4V (video) MOV (quicktime), PDF, or EPub.

What Technical Metadata Does

Technical metadata ensures that the content can work appropriately with the device or software the enduser is using. It is also important for governing technical performance, such as how quickly content is delivered. Technical metadata often impacts the content experiences, such as display or audio quality, or whether certain features are available to users.

1. **Content File Characteristics**. Technical metadata describes content file characteristics, which are often automatically embedded in the file. For example, photo metadata using the **Exif** (exchangeable image file format) standard

encodes information about the resolution of the photo, the make of the camera and settings used.

2. **Format Types**. Technical metadata indicates format type, such as the format of video, audio, or document. It is important to indicate type for media and downloads so content consumers know they can view or play the content. In some cases, formats such as the H.264 format for video use proprietary (patented) technologies, which can trigger licensing concerns and sometimes reduce compatibility with browsers or operating systems.

3. **Embedded Technical Data**. The custom data attribute in HTML5 data- is used to embed data relating to specific content elements. This information is not visible, and intended only for use by local software under the control of the site administrator to support software functions.[67]

Applications of Technical Metadata

Developers use technical metadata to optimize delivery performance and availability to audiences, for example, in responsive web design. Content producers use technical metadata in the creation of composite content.

True to its name, technical metadata can indeed be very technical. Understanding the details of MPEG standards used for audio and video can require an engineering background. But content creators can expect to encounter basic technical metadata relating to file formats and sizes in the course of their work.

Integrated Metadata

Historically, different types of metadata played distinct roles. The structural metadata in a document was separate from the descriptive metadata describing the document, and the administrative metadata governing the document. In modern web content practice, the past separation of roles is giving way to a new practice of integrated metadata. With the rise of greater structure in web content, elements within content can be indicators of both structure and meaning.

A new set of practices for managing web content has evolved known as "intelligent content."[68] The core idea is to break down content into semantically described, structurally independent and measurable units that can be used in multiple contexts. In intelligent content, structural, descriptive and administrative data are aligned and integrated. For example, a piece of a web article might be identified as a `<section>` in HTML (structural metadata). The topic of the section is identified with descriptive metadata. And the section is tagged with analytics to measure how much it is used (administrative metadata). The integrated approach allows different dimensions of web content to be assessed in relation to each other.[69]

[41] "Article Content Model". http://gsa.github.io/Open-And-Structured-Content-Models/models/article-model.html

[42] "Declaring Language in HTML", http://www.w3.org/International/questions/qa-html-language-declarations

[43] "Internationalization Tag Set (ITS) Version 2.0", W3C Recommendation, October 2013, http://www.w3.org/TR/its20/

[44] "Why Use the Language Attribute?" W3C Internationalization, https://www.w3.org/International/questions/qa-lang-why

[45] "Use Metadata", chapter 5 in Jeffrey Pomerantz, *Metadata*. MIT Press, 2015. pp. 117-131

[46] The term *semantic metadata* is used widely, but often informally, without indicating what precisely it refers to. People typically equate semantics with meaning, which should imply a description of the content. But *semantic* as an adjective is often used more broadly to indicate the notion that something can be understood by a computer. The phrase *semantic HTML* refers to **structural** metadata markup, rather than to **descriptive** metadata that indicates what the subject of the content is about.

[47] There is obvious overlap between administrative metadata relating to specific content items, and derived descriptive (behavioral) metadata relating to a body of content. Metadata functions sometimes overlap, where one piece of metadata serves more than one functional role. Metadata affects both management content items individually, and collectively.

[48] Readers interested in the details of copyright in the United States can consult the "Compendium of U.S. Copyright Office Practices, Third Edition", 1,228 pp. December 22, 2014. http://copyright.gov/comp3/

[49] Maureen Whalen, "Rights Metadata Made Simple" in *Introduction to Metadata 3.0*, Getty Museum, 2008.

http://www.getty.edu/research/publications/electronic_publications/intrometadata/rights.pdf

[50] See *Permissions, A Survival Guide* by Susan M. Bielstein (University of Chicago Press)

[51] See, for example, Bloomberg's white paper, "A License to Thrive", http://www.bloomberg.com/distribution/content/uploads/sites/6/2015/06/Content-Licensing-White-Paper.pdf

[52] The issue of images on social media is especially vexing, because some social media platforms will strip out existing metadata that might indicate who created an image.

[53] "AP Content API 2.9" *op. cit.* pp. 15-16.

[54] For example, "Reuters Brand Attribution Guidelines", *Reuters*, http://agency.reuters.com/en/platforms-delivery/reuters-brand-attribution-guidelines.html

[55] "Attribution Guidelines for Yahoo APIs", *Yahoo Developer Network*, https://developer.yahoo.com/attribution/

[56] The "REL" abbreviation for Rights Expression Languages not the same as HTML `rel` attribute (for relationship), although HTML rel can be used with the keyword "license" (e.g., `rel="license"`) to indicate rights.

[57] Creative Commons, "License Versions", https://wiki.creativecommons.org/wiki/License_Versions

[58] *ibid.*

[59] "XMP" on the Creative Commons website, https://wiki.creativecommons.org/wiki/XMP . In this example Creative Commons is working in conjunction with another metadata standard called XMP that is widely used for photos. XMP will be discussed in Chapter 7

[60] The URN ID was shorted in this example to conserve space.

[61] Creative Commons, "Describing Copyright in RDF", http://labs.creativecommons.org/demos/ns/

[62] For an explanation of the meaning of specific terms, consult the Creative Commons documentation.

[63] The details of these licenses are explained on the Open Data Commons website, "Licenses", http://opendatacommons.org/licenses/

[64] "ODRL Version 2.1 Core Model", March 5, 2015, https://www.w3.org/community/odrl/model/2-1/

[65] "IPTC Standards RightsML", http://www.iptc.org/std/RightsML/1.1/RightsML_1.1EP2-spec_1.pdf

[66] IPTC, "RightsML", http://dev.iptc.org/RightsML

[67] "Embedding custom non-visible data with the data-* attributes" in HTML 5.1 W3C Working Draft, October 8, 2015. https://www.w3.org/TR/html51/dom.html#embedding-custom-non-visible-data-with-the-data-*-attributes

[68] Ann Rockley, Charles Cooper, and Scott Abel, *Intelligent Content: A Primer*. XML Press, 2015.

[69] An example of how structural and descriptive metadata can be integrated and combined with detailed information about authorship is offered by an approach called Scholarly HTML. While the approach has been developed specifically for the needs of online scholarly publishing, the principles used in the approach are applicable to web content in general. See "What is Scholarly HTML?" http://scholarly.vernacular.io/

Examples of Metadata as Applied to Content and Media Formats

Metadata can describe a range of content and media formats. Content characteristics can be based on the media, how it is consumed, and the platform on which it is hosted.

Now that we have discussed different functions that metadata plays, let's examine how common metadata attributes are used for text (articles) and for time-based media (videos and podcasts). We'll also discuss back-end data: how web metadata is related to transactional business metadata.

Article metadata

Web articles and blog posts commonly use the following attributes:

- Type (e.g., article or blog)
- Title
- Description
- Site name
- Publication date and time
- Modification date and time
- Tag or keywords
- Aggregate rating
- Word count
- Related links.

It is also possible to include additional metadata concerning entities discussed in the article.

Three different standards are frequently used to describe articles: Dublin Core, schema.org, and Open Graph (each will be discussed later in `Chapter 7`). Since different computer services use different protocols to access the attributes, producers of content may create metadata involving all three standards to describe an article. Such overlap in descriptions allows the content to be used in a wide range of contexts.

Web Media or Digital Asset Metadata

Unlike articles, digital assets such as audio, video and photos can't rely heavily on words in the text for the content to be understood and used. If there is no a transcript associated with an audio or video item, audiences can't learn much about what is specifically mentioned in the item unless metadata is provided indicating the subject matter.

With digital assets, the content and format are intertwined. Metadata plays an important role in the discovery and use of digital assets, both within organizations, and by audiences using browsers and apps. Two of the most popular kinds of web media content are videos placed on YouTube, and podcasts distributed through iTunes. In both cases, the companies hosting the distribution channel (Google/Alphabet and Apple respectively) specify the metadata attributes to use for the content.

- **YouTube Video**

YouTube relies on title, description and tags to describe the content. A thumbnail image provides a pictorial representation of the content. Video contributors can provide information about the date and location of the recording. YouTube allows various forms of annotation such as speech bubbles and notes that give the YouTube search engine more information about what the video relates to. YouTube exposes additional contextual metadata about the video in its API, such as the channel and comments and ratings activity.

- **iTunes Podcast Metadata**

iTunes organizes podcasts into a channel (the series of related podcasts) and items (individual episodes). The channel metadata includes a title, author, summary, thumbnail image, explicitness rating, category (according to Apple's categories), and a user-generated rating. Items have titles, a duration, a file type and size, a date published, and a summary, with popularity being a user-generated attribute.

Popular publishing and syndication channels such as YouTube and iTunes have comparatively few mandatory metadata requirements. When creating digital assets that might be published on many online channels, it is useful to capture more detailed metadata relating to these digital assets, so that they can be available for channels that recognize and can utilize the metadata. Digital asset management systems offer varying degrees of support for and compliance with administrative, descriptive, structural, rights, and technical metadata standards.

Transactional Business Metadata

What is the relationship between metadata for web content, and other kinds of data that businesses manage in their operations? Content requirements should consider how web content metadata will be coordinated with business data managed in transactional IT systems.[70]

Business data is derived from metadata describing and tracking business operations, in contrast to metadata that concerns web content. While these two kinds of metadata generally support different systems and organizational goals, they frequently intersect. It is important therefore they can be mapped to one another. Some key points:

1. **Content and Business Metadata are Different but Related**.

Business metadata describes raw data about activities and may be formalized in a *master data management* (MDM) program. Business metadata is not directly associated with any content type, but often appears in audience-facing content. For example, an ecommerce site may show "availability" or "estimated delivery time" based on the inventory levels.

2. **Product Information Common to Both**.

The most common area of overlap between business and content metadata concerns product information. Organizations may use a tool known as a *product information management* (PIM) system to store descriptive information about their products as structured data in a central location. These descriptions need to be aligned with content metadata so that it can be integrated easily.

3. **Audience Segments Should be Mapped to Marketing and Customer Segments**.

Another dimension of overlap between content and business metadata concerns how customers are segmented. Audience segmentation used in content metadata is most often based on audience needs and interests, while customer segments in business metadata can be based on the scoring of behavioral characteristics such as purchase history. Content analytics can provide deeper insights when the relationship between these two dimensions is clear.

---

[70] Companies use many different transactional IT systems. An example would be an ecommerce platform that supports online ordering, such as SAP Hybris.

Part II. How Metadata Works

We mentioned in Part I that metadata addresses several different levels:

1. The content item
2. The entities in the content item
3. The attributes of entities
4. The values of those attributes.

All that information needs to be encoded, so that computers can understand how content items relate to each other, what entities mean precisely, and how to compare and contrast descriptions made in different places.

Encoding involves four different dimensions:

1. **Data exchange formats**, or markup languages
2. **Data structures**, or metadata schemas
3. **Data values**, or the specific words or numeric values used to describe attributes
4. Data value **formatting and standardization**, or the way values are written to be machine-intelligible.

Figure IIa

Four Key Dimensions of Metadata Encoding

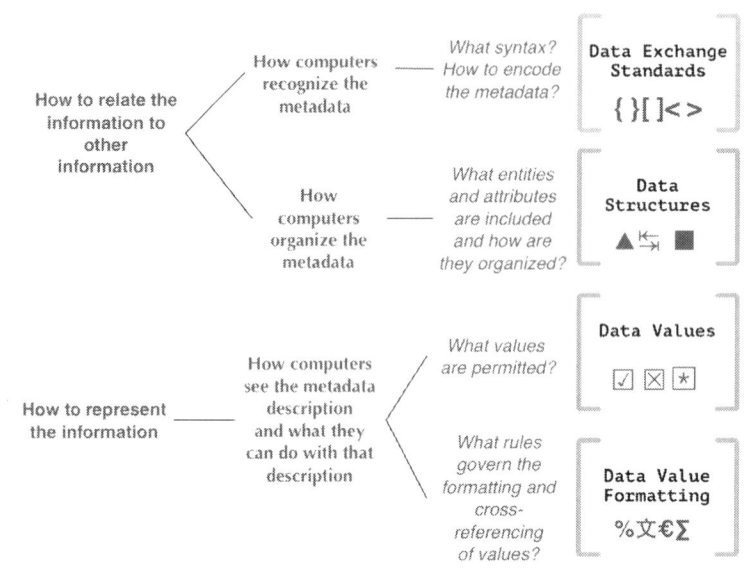

How to relate the information to other information
- How computers recognize the metadata — What syntax? How to encode the metadata? → **Data Exchange Standards** { }[ ]< >
- How computers organize the metadata — What entities and attributes are included and how are they organized? → **Data Structures** ▲⇆ ■

How to represent the information
- How computers see the metadata description and what they can do with that description
  - What values are permitted? → **Data Values** ☑ ☒ ★
  - What rules govern the formatting and cross-referencing of values? → **Data Value Formatting** % 文 € Σ

We will address each of these topics in depth. They are layers of metadata description. The core layers, affecting what is described, relate to the data structures and data values used. The two other layers, the data exchange standards, and data value formatting, affect how the metadata is described, especially so that it is optimally useful for computers.

The data exchange standards affect how metadata is expressed. It may seem difficult and confusing to people who don't have a background in coding, especially since a range of approaches are used. We'll look at data exchange standards first, since it provides a basis for the rest of the metadata description.

Chapter 6. Data Exchange Standards / Metadata Markup Formats

CHAPTER PREVIEW

Data exchange standards, also known as metadata markup formats, enable computers to process metadata that's within a computer file such as a web page. These kinds of standards or formats are often referred to as the syntax used for metadata. Like syntax used in natural language, computer syntax provides rules about the order of items and their punctuation that allows others decipher the message. By adhering to a common syntax, different computers are able to communicate with one another and exchange the information encoded in the metadata. Web content metadata relies on several major data exchange standards:

XML (Extensible Markup Language)

HTML Data Formats, specifically **microformats**, **microdata**, and **RDFa**

JSON (Javascript Object Notation) and **JSON-LD** (JSON Linked Data)

These formats are alternatives, and are sometimes in competition with each other, seeking to become more popular than other formats. In many cases metadata in one format can be converted into another format. Each format offers strengths and weaknesses, generally involving a tradeoff between simplicity, flexibility, and precision. Some formats are optimized for a single purpose. Microdata, for example, was purpose-built to use with schema.org metadata used by search engines. Other formats, such as XML and JSON, can be used for a diverse range of metadata. Flexibility sometimes entails complexity (in the case of XML), while simple standards with generic capabilities (such as offered by JSON) can have limited access to more specialized capabilities, resulting in the need to extend the standard, such as happened with the development of JSON-LD.

Why Markup Matters

An issue of great concern to computers, though of less interest to most humans, is how to exchange information from one computer system to another. An important role of metadata is facilitating the exchange of information between different sources. *Data exchange standards* exist so that different systems and applications can access metadata information wherever it may be.

A data exchange standard provides the *syntax* governing how metadata is encoded. It is the *markup language* used to describe the metadata. Data exchange standards tell developers how to format the metadata code correctly. They are sometimes referred to as the *serialization format* (serialization refers to how data is stored in computer systems).

The syntax of a markup language provides rules for encoding the content. But the syntax must rely on something called a *metadata schema* to specify the meaning of the content, as we will see in `Chapter 7`. In many cases, an individual data exchange standard can be used to encode numerous different metadata schemas.

A data exchange format permits content to be used with any computer system: it is not dependent on the system's procedural language such as JavaScript or PHP. Some syntaxes, due to their design characteristics or the body of code libraries available, are easier for developers to use in specific circumstances. There are many different format standards available to represent data. The three most commonly used for general purpose web content are **XML**, **HTML data formats**, and **JSON**.

Having some familiarity with markup formats is valuable because these dramatically influence what the metadata looks like when it is encoded.[71] The exact same metadata information can look quite different in different markup formats. Knowing some basics about markup formats will allow you to spot what information is being described when you encounter it in the source code, such as the **view source** in a web browser.

---

[71] This chapter provides only a brief survey of data exchange standards. Non-technical readers wanting more detailed instruction on this topic should follow the links to tutorial articles referenced in the footnotes. Technical readers needing

more specific information about coding implementation should refer to the standards documentation online.

XML

XML is common name for the Extensible Markup Language. It is the original metadata markup language for online content, defined soon after the World Wide Web took off in the 1990s. It's a widely used data exchange format, and used for metadata of all kinds.

What XML is

In the words of the W3C, XML is "a simple text-based format for representing structured information: documents, data, configuration, books, transactions, invoices, and much more."[72]

XML is similar in appearance to HTML, with an opening and closing tag in angled brackets surrounding the value. HTML and XML share a common ancestry. But while HTML is a procedural markup indicating how to display content, XML typically only indicates the meaning of the content, not how to display it.

XML markup organizes content into a hierarchical tree that resembles the outline of an essay, but without the bullets or numbering. XML tags are known as *elements*, which define the structure of the content and indicate its meaning. Elements are nested within one another to define a hierarchy of information, moving from broader to narrower. One can also optionally add *attributes* to elements, to refine the meaning indicated.[73] The general pattern of an XML element is as follows:

```
<element-name attribute-name="attribute-value"
/>
```

XML is sometimes referred to as a *metalanguage* because it can be used to define other computer languages. XML markup is used to define many international metadata standards, as well as custom, proprietary metadata standards. XML markup is also the basis of various data transformation protocols that aren't directly associated with metadata.

> *"XML is an alphabet for computers and as everyone traveling to Europe knows, knowing the alphabet doesn't mean you can speak Italian or French."*[74]
>
> -- Business Week *March 18 2002*

Where XML is Used

XML can represent either regular data stored in databases, or narrative content stored as documents. XML is the native format of some content repositories and databases. A web-oriented image format called Scalable Vector Graphics (SVG) is based on XML, and metadata can be embedded within an SVG file.[75]

XML is especially popular to mark up content that will be assembled into large documents, such as books, training manuals, and product documentation. Such content may need to exist in both a downloadable or embedded electronic version, as well as a web-accessible version.

XML is often used to store content that will be incorporated in web content. For example, one can subscribe to a feed of weather forecast data in the XML format from a data provider such as Accuweather. Such a feed might be incorporated by a publisher into their online content.

Non-technical content producers are most likely to encounter XML with RSS feeds.[76]

When and Why XML is Used

XML is designed for machine readability of content, and is not optimized for human readability.

1. **XML Stores Raw Content that can be Transformed into Different Formats**. XML stores content in as raw text that is independent of presentation. XML needs to be converted into HTML or another form of presentation such as a PDF, or into another data format. Specific fragments of text can be retrieved and changed. These characteristics make XML flexible.

2. **XML is Highly Specific and Precise**. XML markup can indicate many details, such as whether information is mandatory or not. It can define default values for attributes, as well as impose constraints on those values. It can

indicate the sequence for elements, or mandate that values must be chosen from a specific list. Because these features are built-in, XML is useful in situations where data precision and quality are paramount.

3. **XML can Involve More Work and be Slower**. XML markup can be verbose and sometimes complex. Some developers consider it as less agile than alternative data exchange formats.

Example of XML

This short fragment of an XML file illustrates some core features of the syntax. The code example is from an introductory article explaining XML on the *IBM developerWorks* website.[77] As the example illustrates, the XML syntax is very similar looking to HTML syntax.

```
<?xml version="1.0" encoding="UTF-8"?>  ❶
<recipe type="dessert">  ❷
    <recipename cuisine="american" servings="1">Ice Cream Sundae</recipename>  ❸
    <preptime>5 minutes</preptime>  ❹
</recipe>  ❺
```

❶ Declaration indicating this is an XML file.

❷ Beginning of entry for a recipe. All information belongs to the recipe entry until the closing tag. In this example, two elements are nested within the recipe element:

126

<recipename> and <preptime>.

❸ The value of the <recipename> element is "Ice Cream Sunday". This element has two attributes: cuisine and serving which have their own values. These attributes can be used to sort information: e.g., find all recipe names where cuisine is American.

❹ This element doesn't have any attributes within it, unlike the previous one.

❺ Closing tag for entry.

---

[72] "XML Essentials"
https://www.w3.org/standards/xml/core
[73] The term *attribute* here refers to its syntactical role of being an attribute (modifier or qualifier) of an XML element, rather than to a semantic role of being an attribute (property) of an entity. This is another case where the same term is used in slightly different ways in different contexts. From a functional perspective, a syntax attribute used for encoding XML metadata is different from an entity attribute that describes characteristics of a thing conceptually, even though sometimes the syntax attribute may be used to encode the semantic attribute of an entity in specific implementations of metadata.

Because attributes are optional in XML, many elements won't have syntax attributes.

[74] Quoted in Liyang Yu, *A Developers Guide to the Semantic Web*, Springer, second edition, p. 91

[75] http://www.w3.org/TR/SVG/metadata.html

[76] XML is generally simple to read, but if you aren't familiar with XML you may encounter some strings of characters that look odd. XML has restrictions concerning the use of five characters: the ampersand, the less-than sign, the greater-than sign, the apostrophe, and the quotation mark. These character need to be encoded in a special manner, so that a quotation mark is written as ".

[77] Example from Kay Whatley, "XML basics for new users", *IBM developerWorks*, February 24, 2009
`http://www.ibm.com/developerworks/library/x-newxml/`

HTML Data Formats

Standard HTML markup only provides limited support to describe and exchange metadata. However, it can be enhanced to include descriptive metadata about entities, and provide identifying metadata about administrative elements such as author, and about structural elements such as tables. Enhanced HTML markup is referred to as HTML data formats. The major kinds of HTML data formats are **microformats**, **microdata**, and **RDFa**, each of which will be described shortly.

While the details of each HTML format varies, the general approach each uses to encode metadata is broadly similar. They often are used to address similar kinds of content, though are not exactly equivalent alternatives. Microformats are the simplest but most limited. The microdata format and RDFa format in many cases offer equivalent features, though the RDFa format offers additional flexibility not available in microdata format.

When and Why HTML Data Formats are Used

Since nearly all web content is published using HTML markup, using HTML markup for metadata as well offers certain benefits.

- **HTML Data Formats Integrate Content and Metadata**. The philosophy behind HTML data formats is to annotate content with metadata to give it more structure. Both publishers and consumers of web content recognize that much web content lacks structure, making it hard to index and manage. HTML data formats provide a way to enhance the meaning of content for the benefit of computer applications and people using these applications.

HTML data formats permit both human- and machine-readable content to be published in tandem, so that one version of the content can serve both readers and IT systems. This integrated approach is different from the approach of other data exchange formats, where a file containing the metadata may be separate from the content audiences view.

HTML Data Formats are Sometimes Simpler. The advantage of HTML data formats is that the content remains in HTML, so no alternate data exchange format is required. This removes procedural and programming tasks involved with converting formats or managing multiple formats. The workflow can also be potentially simpler, if authors can simply highlight entities requiring metadata, instead of having to enter that information as a separate task. However, HTML data formats are not always simple to implement when content is complex.

Microformats

Microformats are "a set of simple, open data formats built upon existing and widely adopted standards", in the words of microformats.org.[78]

Microformats were the first HTML data exchange format designed to share information on a web page with other applications.[79] Because of its simplicity and harmony with existing web standards, it has enjoyed wide use. Google and Facebook recognize personal information encoded in microformats, and various food related websites and applications recognize recipes encoded with microformats.

Microformat specifications are recommended practices rather than formal standards. They reflect common practices rather than being official standards created by standards bodies. For example the microformat for contact information draws on the vCard format that is widely used in address book applications, which can indicate, among other things:

- Full, formatted name
- Structured name (e.g, given name, family name, prefix and suffix)
- Email address
- URL
- Structured address (e.g, street address, locality, region, postal code, country name)

- Birthday.

Microformats are used pervasively, though they are less dominant now than they once were. Strictly speaking, microformats not only support data exchange, but also encompass features that organize what the data means. Unlike other data exchange formats discussed in this chapter that can exchange data about all kinds of entities, microformats are limited in the kinds of entities they can represent. Microformats are sometimes an alternative to the other HTML data formats we will discuss, though microformats have a more limited scope and are not fully equivalent to these other formats.

How Microformats Work

Microformats place *attributes* inside existing HTML *elements* to indicate the meaning of HTML content that audiences see.[80] We'll see an example of what that looks like shortly. But first, let's consider some design aspects of microformats and their consequences. Microformats combine syntax guidelines with guidelines on how to describe entities. The simple design of microformats means it is less powerful and flexible than other data exchange formats. Microformats can only describe certain attributes and certain entities. Other data exchange formats can work with more than one schema, and can as a result describe a wide range of entities.

Microformat syntax relies on two core HTML attributes: `class` and `rel`.

`class` Attribute

Microformats use the HTML class attribute that is typically used for CSS styling to indicate entity type and attributes. A root class wraps the entire description to indicate the type of entity. The attributes and values associated with the entity are commonly expressed within a `<div>` or `<span>` tag. The consistent use of class names to describe common attributes enables other applications to find and harvest this information.

`rel` Attribute

The `rel` (relationship) attribute can indicate what a link refers to. It is most commonly used for license information: for example, linking to a URL such as a creative commons license.

Applications of Microformats

A number of microformats exist, though some never gained wide usage, or have become overtaken by developments in web standards. The most widely used are:

- `hCard` for contact information
- `hCalendar` for event information
- `hNews` for news articles
- `hProduct` for product information

- `hReview` for product reviews
- `hRecipes` for recipes

Each microformat focuses a specific type of entity, and provides various properties and sub-properties to describe the entity. One can combine different microformats in a single description.

A newer version of the specification (microformats2) uses a hyphen to refer to the microformat (e.g., `h-card` instead of hCard). This reflects a slight change in syntax of using single letter prefix followed by a hyphen to indicate the type of data:

- `h-*` for "root classes" focused on entities such as the h-card for personal contact information
- `p-*` for plain text properties such as `p-label`
- `u-*` for URL properties such as `u-email`
- `dt-*` for data-time properties such as `dt-start`

Example of a Microformat

The following example shows markup for an event using the revised microformat syntax.[81]

```
<div class="h-event"> ❶
    <h1 class="p-name">Microformats Meetup</h1>❷
    <p>From
```

```
        <time class="dt-start" datetime="2013-06-
30 12:00">30<sup>th</sup> June 2013,
12:00</time> ❸
        to <time class="dt-end" datetime="2013-
06-30 18:00">18:00</time>
        at <span class="p-location">Some bar in
SF</span></p> ❹
    <p class="p-summary">Get together and
discuss all things microformats-related.</p>
</div>
```

❶ Indicates event-related information presented within the `<div>` element. Attribute names are typically announced by the use of the `class` attribute. The entire entry within the opening and closing `<div>` elements refers to an event.

❷ The title (within the `<h1>` element) that is associated with the event. The value for the title is "Microformats Meetup". The existing HTML content is annotated with `"p-name"` attribute to indicate that the HTML content refers to a title within an event.

❸ Information about the start time of the event is presented within the `<time>` element. A machine-readable version of this information is presented within the `datetime` attribute.

❹ In this example, the location information is not precise, though more precise location information can be specified using microformats.

Microdata

Microdata is another alternative for making data within HTML content machine-readable. Microdata is "a mechanism allows machine-readable data to be embedded in HTML documents in an easy-to-write manner".[82] It is an extension of HTML5, and was created by the Web Hypertext Application Technology Working Group, the group instrumental in the development of HTML5.

While similar-sounding to microformats, and sometimes confused with it, microdata was designed to overcome the coverage limitations of microformats. Microdata can be used with various metadata schemas, but in practice it is used mostly with a standard called schema.org, which will be discussed in `Chapter 8`.

How Microdata Works

Microdata annotates HTML content using nested groupings of "name-value pairs." A simple example that follows illustrates microdata in practice.[83]

```
<div itemscope>   <p>My name is <span itemprop="name">Elizabeth</span>.</p> </div>
```

The content between the `<div>` tags is a content item that has microdata. The content item has an attribute called name that has a value of Elizabeth. Hence, we can infer that the content item refers to someone named Elizabeth.[84]

Microdata generally involves using a schema (a standard defining what attribute names mean), though that is not formally required. Inclusion of a schema definition however is essential for outside parties such as search engines to understand unambiguously to what the information relates.

The microdata syntax refers to entities being as *items*. An item is announced by the phrase itemscope. The attributes of an entity are indicated by itemprop (for item property).

To indicate the kind of entity being defined, an itemscope may have an itemtype (a formal entity type), which specifies the schema involved and entity defined by the schema. This information helps machines understand the meaning of the property being expressed. The itemtype will have as its value a link to schema online. If the entity has a permanent unique online identity such as product ID number, this can optionally be indicated with the itemid.

Use of HTML5 Elements

Properties are defined within HTML elements. These elements may be structural block elements such as paragraph <p>. Items but most often are defined within non-structural in-line elements such as <div> and <span> since the properties describing an item may be located anywhere within the body of text.

Microdata can be used with several semantic elements introduced in HTML5 to enhance machine-readability:[85]

- The meter element `<meter>` to express numeric values within a range, which can contain a value attribute, and optional values for min and max, and high, low and optimum.

- The time element `<time>`, which can contain a `datetime` attribute

- The data element `<data>`, which contains a value attribute

- A definition list `<dl>`, which can include different properties associated with an entity.

Microdata Attributes

Microdata indicates global attributes using the following key words:

- `itemscope`, which creates an instance of an entity being described

- `itemtype`, which indicates the kind of entity according to the schema being used (if used, must be a URL)

- `itemid`, which identifies the entity a global identifier (a URL or other machine addressable ID)

- `itemprop`, which indicates that a property of the entity will be identified

- `itemref`, which provides a way to reference other elements containing properties related to items.

Each property of an item is referred to as `itemprop`, and the type of attribute is listed in quotes. The value for each `itemprop` can be listed in several ways:

- As a human-visible *literal* value in the HTML body

- As a `href` link (when the type of `itemprop` is a URL)

- As a machine visible value enclosed in quotes for certain property types such as dates, or as a content value intended for machines.

Example of Microdata

The following example illustrates microdata markup for a video.[86] Much of the markup concerns technical and administrative metadata.

```
<div itemscope
itemtype="http://schema.org/VideoObject"> ❶
<span itemprop="name">Title of video</span>
❷
<span itemprop="description">Video description</span>
```

139

```
<img itemprop="thumbnailUrl"
src="thumbnail1.jpg" alt="thumbnail text"/>
<meta itemprop="uploadDate" content="2015-02-
05T08:00:00+08:00"/> ❸
<meta itemprop="duration" content="PT1M33S" />
<link itemprop="contentUrl"
href="http://www.example.com/video123.flv" />
<link itemprop="embedUrl"
href="http://www.example.com/videoplayer.swf?v
ideo=123" />
<meta itemprop="interactionCount"
content="2347" />
</div>
```

❶ The `itemscope` announces a structured data description contained within a `<div>` element. The `itemtype` indicates that the entity described is a video (`"VideoObject"`).

❷ Each property of the entity is indicated using the attribute `itemprop`. The name of the video is presented within a `<span>` element that will be visible to audiences.

❸ When the video was uploaded is indicated within a `<meta>` element. The data for this property is machine-readable only.

Microdata is mostly used to support search engines. Various search engines provide **structured data testing tools** that reveal what data gets extracted from the body of content by search engines.

Client-side applications such as browsers can extract microdata using the **Microdata DOM API**.[87] It allows JavaScript programs to access the properties in content marked up as microdata.

RDFa

The goals motivating the development of RDFa are similar to other data formats: to get web content creators to annotate a diverse variety of web content so that machines can understand it. RDFa aims to allow any kind of web content to become machine readable and intelligible, without requiring the re-entry of information. As the W3C specification states:

"RDFa Core is a specification for attributes to express structured data in any markup language. The embedded data already available in the markup language (e.g., HTML) can often be reused by the RDFa markup, so that publishers don't need to repeat significant data in the document content."[88]

The RDFa syntax is designed to allow embedding within HTML a data structure called the Resource Description Framework (RDF), which is the **F**ramework to **D**escribe a content **R**esource. The *a* in RDFa refers to putting the RDF data into the attributes of HTML. A scaled down version called RDFa Lite also exists, which is meant to cover most common use cases, while removing some less-used features.

RDFa syntax embeds semantic metadata within attributes of HTML tags. Attributes aren't visible to the audience, but encode a hyperlink indicating the meaning of the attribute. A simple example from the W3C shows how this works.[89]

```
<div vocab="http://xmlns.com/foaf/0.1/"
about="#me">
My name is <span property="name">John
Doe</span> and my blog is called
<a property="homepage"
href="http://example.org/blog/">Understanding
Semantics</a>.
</div>
```

We will assume that the content segment between the `<div>` tags is from an "About Me" page on a blog. The `vocab` attribute indicates that the content is being described using a schema known as **Friend of a Friend** that can describe different aspects of people.[90] This example identifies what's being described using the `"name"` property, with a value of John Doe. We also see a hyperlink that is identified as a homepage about what's being described. The important features to pay attention to at this point are the attributes: the `vocab` (indicating the schema), the `about` (indicating the subject of the description), and the `property` (indicating the kind of attribute being described).

The RDF data structure expresses relationships between entities as three-part statement:

- A **subject** (the entity)

- A **predicate** (a relational verb, also often referred to as a property)

- An **object** (the value of that property associated with that entity).

RDFa can be used with any metadata schema (an organizing framework that will be discussed in Chapter 7), and can accommodate the use of several schemas to describe a block of content. RDF can even combine different sets of data, so that one descriptive statement references two or more different sets of data.

RDFa syntax can be slightly more complex that either microformats or microdata, but is more flexible. Unlike microdata, it can be used with more than one schema at once.

How RDFa Works

RDFa is an extension of HTML5 – it adds additional attributes and features not present in the core HTML5 standard.

RDFa describes data using a pattern known as *triples*. The basic triple pattern expresses the **Entity-Attribute-Value** relationship in the form of **Subject-Property-Object**.[91] Apart from a slight difference in terminology, the most important difference is that the value of an attribute can be either a simple literal value such as word or number, or it can be another entity. When the value is another entity, the value can stand for other values associated with the entity. This is done by declaring the value as a `resource` and including a URL that describes the entity.

RDFa uses several core HTML attributes such as `href` (hyperlink URL), `src` (source URL), `rel` (relationship) and `content`. It adds some additional attributes not present in standard HTML:

- `about`, which indicates the subject
- `vocab`, which indicates the schema or data structure
- `typeof`, which is the entity type as defined by a schema
- `property`, which is an attribute pertaining to the subject described
- `resource`, referring to what is being described, expressed as a href
- `prefix`, which can provide an abbreviation for a referenced schema

Detailed RDFa Example

The following provides and example of RDFa markup for a review of a restaurant.[92] This example illustrates how the description of an entity can refer to other entities. In this example, the review includes mentions of other entities that are described within the description:

- Restaurant (`"itemReviewed"`)

- Rating ("reviewRating")

- Person ("author")

- Organization ("publisher").

```
<div vocab="http://schema.org/"
typeof="Review"> ❶
<div property="itemReviewed"
typeof="Restaurant"> ❷
   <span property="name">Legal Seafood</span>
❸
</div>
<span property="reviewRating"
typeof="http://schema.org/Rating">
   <span property="ratingValue">4</span> ❹
</span> stars - <b>"
   <span property="name">A good seafood place.
</span>" </b>
<span property="author"
typeof="http://schema.org/Person">
   <span property="name">Bob Smith</span>
</span>
<span property="reviewBody">The seafood is
great.</span>   <div property="publisher"
typeof="Organization">
   <meta property="name" content="Washington
Times"> ❺
   </div>
</div>
```

❶ Indicates structured data concerning a review. The vocab attribute indicates the use of metadata schema called schema.org. The typeof attribute indicates the kind of entity being described. In this example, a review is being

145

described using structured data.

❷ The `property` indicates what is being reviewed. The `typeof` indicates that a restaurant is being reviewed.

❸ The "`itemReviewed`" has name of "Legal Seafood", which is visible to audiences.

❹ Another entity associated with the review: the Rating. It has a property called "`ratingValue`" that is a number.

❺ Here is some machine-readable only data contained in the `<meta>`. It indicates that the review was published by an organization (as opposed to an individual) and gives the name of the organization.

In this example, unlike the earlier RDFa example, there is no about attribute. The about attribute in some cases is optional.

RDFa is widely used in HTML content. It largely used to support search engines.

---

[78] "About microformats",
  http://microformats.org/wiki/about

[79] Microformats emerged around 2005 in response to online discussions about how to represent data on webpages. Microformats are a community effort without much formal organizational structure. The central hub for microformats is the website microformats.org.

[80] Fortunately, the syntax of microformats and other HTML data formats (microdata and RDFa) utilizes HTML element attributes to indicate semantic attributes (i.e., the properties) of content items and entities. This makes the relationship between syntax and semantics more straightforward than in XML.

[81] *"h-event"*, Microformats Wiki, http://microformats.org/wiki/h-calendar

[82] "HTML Microdata", W3C Working Group Note, October 29 2013, http://www.w3.org/TR/microdata/

[83] *ibid.*

[84] That the name refers to a person is not explicit, however, since the metadata does not indicate the type of entity being described.

[85] See "HTML Living Standard" https://html.spec.whatwg.org/multipage/microdata.html#microdata-and-other-namespaces

[86] Microdata markup example provided by Google. https://developers.google.com/structured-data/rich-snippets/videos

[87] http://www.w3.org/TR/microdata/#microdata-dom-api

[88] "RDFa Core 1.1 - Third Edition", W3C Recommendation March 17 2015, https://www.w3.org/TR/rdfa-core/

[89] "RDFa Core 1.1 - Third Edition", W3C, http://www.w3.org/TR/rdfa-syntax/

[90] Discussed more in Chapter 8.

[91] RDFa markup often uses the term property to indicate the predicate, so I am using that term here.

[92] RDFa markup example provided by Google. https://developers.google.com/structured-data/rich-snippets/reviews

JSON

JSON is formally known as **JavaScript Object Notation**, and is pronounced "jayson". It is an alternative format to XML. We'll discuss two versions of JSON: standard JSON, and a new variant called JSON-LD designed for semantic metadata, that builds on standard JSON.

What JSON is

JSON is a popular data exchange format. It uses simple formatting rules to allow the portable representation of data. It is similar to XML, but is more streamlined.

Many developers praise the "readability" of JSON, even though the format is designed for machines to consume. They mean that it is easy for developers to read and debug – not that audiences are meant to read JSON data.

Superficially, you notice JSON from its use of square and curly brackets, compared with the angled brackets in HTML and XML.

```
{"pets":[
    {"name":"Spot", "type":"dog"},
    {"name":"Princess", "type":"cat"},
    {"name":"Guppy", "type":"goldfish"}
]}
```

When developers need to provide data as an output for other applications to use, they will often represent the data using JSON.

JSON is derived from JavaScript, though it can be used with any programming language. When used together with HTML, JSON data is presented within a `<script>` tag, which is separate from the body of HTML content.

The metadata contained in JSON is separate from the values presented in the body of the web content itself. JSON metadata sometimes repeats same information contained in the body of the HTML. But it sometimes adds information that may not be explicit in the content.

When and Why JSON is used

JSON has become the dominant data structure to bridge data in stored in different places.

1. Data Portability

JSON is designed to facilitate the movement of data between applications, to make data portable. JSON data is machine-visible only. It is separate from the content presented to audiences. It provides a parallel description of the content intended for machines that can be transformed into HTML for audiences to view.

While JSON, HTML data formats, and XML all allow data to be ported from one context to another, moving data with JSON is often simpler. JSON less oriented to describing documents compared to XML and HTML data formats. It is a pure data format that is designed for parsing. While JSON historically has not been considered a document format, that may be changing. Apple is using JSON for its Apple News Format.[93]

JSON is also the basis for several specialized data exchange formats. GeoJSON is a widely used format to express location data.[94]

2. Client-Server Interaction

JSON's major advantage is that its syntax works well with JavaScript, a computer language used for screen-based interactivity. Users can make requests on screen (the client) and fetch the appropriate information from the server. JSON offers the ability to easily and quickly exchange data between the user and the server. Users can also manipulate fragments of content on screen.

To use JSON data for on-screen display, the values used in the machine-readable JSON file must also be human-readable. As a result, JSON values are most often represented as stings instead of in more precise, machine-readable data types.

Standard JSON

JSON has a hierarchical structure. In JSON, attributes are called *names*. Both the attributes and the text values are indicated within quotation marks. Values that are numbers, or indicate True or False, don't use quotation marks.

Because text is always enclosed within quotation marks, if the text itself uses quotes, these quotes need to be preceded by a backslash, so they are "escaped" and not confused with the quotes surrounding the larger block of text. For example:

> "comments": "Alice recommends \"Harry Potter and the Order of the Phoenix\". "

Groups of related attribute-value pairs that describe an item are enclosed in curly brackets. Ordered lists of items (known as *arrays*, where there can be more than one value for an attribute) are grouped together within square brackets. Curly brackets surround the entire description of an entity.

JSON Example

Here's an example of metadata encoded in standard JSON that would be passed to a client.[95] The example shows how metadata can support different user needs. The price that will be displayed on the screen for the product will depend on the quantity that the user selects.

```
{                       ❶
    "product": {        ❷
        "name": "Widget",    ❸
        "company": "ACME, Inc",
        "partNumber": "7402-129",
        "prices": [     ❹
            { "minQty": 1, "price": 12.49 },   ❺
            { "minQty": 10, "price": 9.99 },
            { "minQty": 50, "price": 7.99 }
        ]
    }
}
```

❶ All entities described will be within curly brackets {}. This is the root.

❷ The entity is "`product`" and the description of it follows within curly brackets.

❸ The first of name-value pairs, indicating the attribute and value for the entity. The pairs are separated by a colon.

❹ Here the attribute "`prices`" contains more than one value. The syntax indicates a list by using square brackets `[]`.

❺ The values in the list contain compound values. These are expressed using curly brackets, where each name-value pair is separated by a comma.

JSON and XML: What are the Differences?

JSON and XML are largely equivalent, even though each was originally developed to serve different purposes. Both organize information according to a hierarchy. JSON is more oriented to representing structured data, while XML is more focused on describing documents. As a practical matter each can do what the other can do, with a few limitations, but how they represent metadata is slightly different.

One key difference concerns the levels of information. XML has three levels of information: the element or tag (indicating what's described), one or more optional attributes (modifiers of what's described), and the value of the element. For example, in XML, if you want to indicate that the American English description of an article, it might look like this:

```
<description lang="en-us">Research Findings on Arctic Warming</description>
```

JSON only has two levels: the key (what's described) and a value. That means that in JSON the information described by XML elements and attributes need to be listed separately, like this:

```
{ "description":
    {      "@lang":"en-us",
           "#text":"Research Findings on Arctic Warming"
           }
    }
```

This is only an illustrative example.[96] Alternative implementations are possible.

JSON-LD

JSON-LD is an enhanced version of JSON. The *LD* in JSON-LD stands for **L**inked **D**ata, a form of semantic metadata. Standard JSON is forward-compatible with JSON-LD, so that it can be converted into JSON-LD when some additional context information is added.

JSON-LD looks a lot like standard JSON. The major difference is that it declares several elements using an @ sign. The most important of these are:

- `@context` (declares a description, and optionally can provide a reference to an abbreviation of the metadata schema being used, similar to the RDFa "prefix")
- `@vocab` (a reference to the schema used)
- `@id` (the subject being described)
- `@type` (the entity type)
- `@value` (the value of an entity)

Unlike standard JSON, JSON-LD recognizes additional *data types* such as dates.

JSON-LD is an alternative format to RDFa. JSON-LD provides an RDF statement into a format JavaScript developers can use. JSON-LD has an **API** to support the retrieval and manipulation of data for various applications.[97] JSON-LD can be integrated with web components.[98]

JSON-LD Example

Here is a JSON-LD example for an event.[99] The basic syntax is similar to standard JSON. It provides another example of where one entity ("Event") makes reference to another entity ("Place"). None of the values in the syntax are visible to audiences.[100]

```
<script type="application/ld+json"> ❶
{ ❷
   "@context": "http://schema.org", ❸
   "@type": "Event", ❹
   "name": "Example Band goes to San Francisco",
   "startDate" : "2013-09-14T21:30",
   "url" : "http://example.com/tour-dates.html",
   "location" : { ❺
      "@type" : "Place", ❻
      "sameAs" : "http://www.hi-dive.com",
      "name" : "The Hi-Dive",
      "address" : "7 S. Broadway, Denver, CO 80209"
   } ❼
} ❽
</script> ❾
```

❶ The `<script>` element in HTML announces that a JSON-LD file is included.

❷ Start of the JSON-LD description.

❸ The `"@context"` announces the schema used, in this case schema.org.

❹ The "@type" indicates the entity type being described, which is an Event.

❺ The location contains a compound value, which is indicated by {}.

❻ The location is a different type of entity, indicated by "@type":"Place".

❼ End of the description for the Place.

❽ End of the description for the Event.

❾ Closing HTML element indicating boundary of JSON-LD file.

---

[93] "Apple News Format"
https://developer.apple.com/library/ios/documen tation/General/Conceptual/Apple_News_Format_Ref /index.html#//apple_ref/doc/uid/TP40015408- CH79-SW1
[94] "The GeoJSON Format Specification",
http://geojson.org/geojson-spec.html

[95] Example from Google Web Kit developer site. "JSON", http://www.gwtproject.org/doc/latest/DevGuideCodingBasicsJSON.html

[96] For examples of the conversion process, see Stefan Goessner, "Converting Between XML and JSON", O'Reilly XML.com, May 31, 2006. http://www.xml.com/pub/a/2006/05/31/converting-between-xml-and-json.html

[97] http://www.w3.org/TR/json-ld-api/

[98] "Creating semantic sites with Web Components and JSON-LD" *Google Developers*, https://developers.google.com/web/updates/2015/03/creating-semantic-sites-with-web-components-and-jsonld?hl=en

[99] JSON-LD example provided by Google https://developers.google.com/structured-data/rich-snippets/events

[100] JSON-LD metadata will often repeat content shown to audiences that's written in HTML. One drawback of JSON-LD is that works against the "DRY" principle of Don't Repeat Yourself.

Data Standards for Semantic Metadata Compared

According to the WebDataCommons project's annual crawl of websites globally, about 38% of all websites use structured data — either microdata, RDFa, JSON-LD, or microformats. The project reports that as of October 2016: "Approximately 2.5 million of these websites use Microdata, 2.1 million websites employ JSON-LD, and 938 thousand websites use RDFa. Microformats are used by over 1.6 million websites within the crawl."[101]

Use of RDFa, microdata, and JSON-LD to express the properties of entities in web content is growing.[102] Each of these metadata formats is largely interchangeable, and each is used widely, so it is helpful to develop an understanding of how they compare.

Documentation for each of these formats contains many specifics relating to how to describe entities using these properties. We can compare the property keywords used in each approach. This is only a high level comparison: refer to the documentation for precise implementation details and qualifications. Some of the keywords are optional to use, and some descriptive elements are optional to express.

	Microdata	**RDFa**	**JSON-LD**
How to indicate the schema used	(Declared by `itemtype`)	`vocab`	`@vocab`
How to indicate the subject	`itemid`	`about`	`@id`
How to indicate the type of entity	`itemtype`	`typeof`	`@type`
How to indicate the predicate or property	`itemprop`	`property`	(Declared through `@type`)
How to indicate the value	`content`	`resource, content`	`@value`
How to abbreviate references to schema or schema entity type		`prefix`	`@context`

[101] "Web Data Commons - RDFa, Microdata, Embedded JSON-LD, and Microformats Data Sets - October 2016", `http://webdatacommons.org/structureddata/2016-10/stats/stats.html`

[102] As mentioned earlier, microformats are much more limited in the range of entities that can be described, and are becoming less popular. XML can be used to describe the properties of entities, but is not as popular for that purpose as XML markup supports a much broader range of applications, and hence more complex to use.

Syntax Diversity

For many people, the diversity of syntaxes available to encode metadata is bewildering. The nature of data exchange means that metadata is often converted from one format into another. You may need to accept metadata from one IT system encoded in one format, manage it within your own IT system another format, and possibly export it to yet a different format so that it will be easy for others to use in their IT systems. Ideally, however, you will work primarily with one format that you will get to know in some depth.[103] Believe it or not, there are even more data exchange formats used to manage metadata that we haven't covered.[104] But most readers will work with one of the formats addressed in this chapter.

---

[103] There are conflicting opinions concerning the advisability of embedding a mixture metadata formats in content. In principle machines should be capable of recognizing different formats within a content item, and publishers may have sound reasons to implement multiple formats. However, some developers report problems when trying to get such mixed code validated.

[104] Some publishers who work with large volumes of metadata choose simpler specialized data formats such as Turtle or N3 when encoding the metadata, and then convert the metadata into a more web-friendly format.

Chapter 7. Data Structures, or Metadata Schemas

CHAPTER PREVIEW

Whereas data exchange standards concern *how* to express metadata with code, data structures concern *what* the metadata can describe. Data structures are also known as metadata schemas, and I will use both terms. They define the properties that can be used with different content types and entity types. Data structures are a blueprint of all the metadata attributes associated with your content, indicating the relationships between these attributes. For example, content might discuss various universities, and universities have locations. A metadata schema could specify a university as entity type, and indicate specific attributes of that entity type such as its location, which might include a city and region. By using such a data structure, a computer will understand that a city mentioned is associated with a university mentioned in the content. Metadata schema standards allow different publishers to describe their metadata in a consistent way. Three of the most important general purpose data structure standards are **schema.org**, **Dublin Core**, and the **Open Graph protocol**. Schema.org, developed by search engine companies such as Google, is used to indicate to search engines the meaning of entities in the content. Dublin Core, an older metadata schema, has influenced many other metadata schemas used for web content. The Open Graph protocol, developed by Facebook, supports the use of content on social networks.

In addition to these general purpose metadata schemas, specialized schemas can be useful for web content. Examples include **FOAF** or Friend of a Friend (for personal information) and **XMP** or Extensible Metadata Platform (for photos and other digital assets).

Many metadata schemas are available, but publishers are not restricted to using one only. They can use several together. Using existing schemas is the best option for sharing metadata with others. But if an existing schema does not address your needs, it is possible to extend existing schemas, and even to create one's own schema, though that is not prudent option for most web publishers.

How Structures or Schemas Supply Meaning to Metadata

Metadata fundamentally is about describing what content and entities mean. The meaning is provided through what's known as a *data structure* or a *metadata schema*.[105]

What is a data structure or metadata schema? Data structures or metadata schemas define the *kinds of attributes* available to describe an entity, though they generally do not specify what specific values to use.[106] They are a model of the properties of entities associated with a topical or functional domain.[107] For example, if you create content that discusses personal details of celebrities, you might want a metadata schema that can specify these personal details, such as who someone's ex-spouse is, or perhaps their favorite movie.

Data structures work in concert with data exchange standards such as XML, RDFa or JSON. The data structure provides the conceptual model of the metadata (the *semantics*), while the data exchange standard provides the instructions for how to encode the conceptual model (the *syntax*). In many cases, a data structure can be encoded using any one of several data exchange standards. In some cases, the data structure relies on certain features available in a specific data exchange standard to enforce how concepts in the model are understood. For example, in XML one might be able to implement a data structure that indicates whether an attribute is mandatory or not, while HTML data formats do not offer this feature. In summary, a data structure encompasses a conceptual model of the data, guidelines relating to entities and attributes, and sometimes strict rules that are enforced through the data exchange format.

Data structures are a core concept in metadata, but confusingly the concept is referred to by many different names. In addition being known as metadata schemas, they are referred to by other names as well. Sometimes they called *the data model*. They are also sometimes called *vocabularies*, though that phrase can easily be confused with the concept of controlled vocabularies, which will be discussed later. To avoid possible confusion between the role of schemas and the role of descriptive values, we will generally avoid using the phase *vocabularies* to refer to metadata schemas. We will use the terms data structures and schemas interchangeably in this discussion, as these are the most common names used to refer to how metadata entities and attributes are defined.

---

[105] Both terms are widely used. Since the various standards we'll be discussing refer to themselves as schemas and/or structures, using both terms is unavoidable, if inelegant.

[106] Some schemas enforce business rules relating to values. Some schemas limit the values of certain attributes using something called enumerations, discussed later in Chapter 7. But for the most part, the publisher will be responsible for making decisions about the specific values to include.

[107] This book will mostly focus on schemas for topical domains. Schemas can sometimes include functional aspects such business rules, or procedural instructions.

Why Data Structures are Important

Data structures can be thought of as a plan of what metadata to capture, and how it should be organized.

A data structure defines what the metadata represents. It describes what the entity pertains to, much like a dictionary defines the meaning of a word. The entity definition may indicate what is included and excluded, and perhaps instructions on situations where you should use the entity.

Unlike a dictionary, however, a data structure is just not a flat list of words with definitions. A data structure expresses rules for metadata descriptions. For example, which attributes can be used to describe an entity? That will depend on the type of entity, or the *class* that the entity belongs to.[108] A class can be related to other classes that are either more general (using fewer, more generic attributes) or more specific (using additional specialized attributes). The relationships between various classes in a data structure provide a rich set of information for computers, which can expect the whether properties are associated with an entity.

Data structures also help machines understand what attributes refer to. Suppose a computer encounters an attribute called "issue date". What format for the data should the issue date be in? What entity type or types are associated with an issue date? A data structure provides a specification covering precisely what details mean and are required.

The Value of Public Metadata Schemas

It is possible to create a *proprietary* metadata schema for one's own private use. Such an approach will help to coordinate metadata internally, but it won't let one share metadata with others easily.

When a metadata schema is made *public*, it can be assigned a *namespace* that anyone can use. A namespace is a fixed online address (known as a URI) that provides a description of the data structure. Namespaces are declared in the metadata with the address and optionally, with a short name of a namespace. Computers (and content designers hoping to share and reuse information expressed in metadata) can then understand what the entities and attributes refer to. This allows different parties (organizations and machines) to exchange data easily, without needing to refer to special instructions. Data becomes discoverable.

Public metadata schemas help to break down informational silos by allowing individuals and organizations to access metadata that's published by anyone using the public schema. *Linked data* offers different publishers the ability to share metadata with each other, and even reference each other's metadata within their own metadata.[109]

Published metadata schemas let content publishers know what they need to do to conform with the standard, so that their metadata can be accessed and reused easily.

[108] Not all metadata schemas designate entity types that restrict which attributes are allowed, but entity typing is a feature of many of the most important schemas.

[109] A formal definition of linked data involves various technical criteria that are outside the scope of this discussion. Tim Berners-Lee outlined his criteria in a well-known 2007 article called "Linked Data", available at `https://www.w3.org/DesignIssues/LinkedData.html`. The linked data concept applies to all kinds of data, not just web content published for general audiences. For those involved with web content, an important concept in linked data is that one's metadata is shared with other publishers. Not only does one publish content with metadata values, but some of the values are hyperlinks to other related metadata. This can allows computers to compare metadata between different publishers to determine if they are referring to the same entity, and if they are, discover additional information available in the metadata of the linked websites.

General Purpose Metadata Schemas

Three general-purpose metadata schemas are schema.org, Dublin Core, and the Open Graph protocol.

Schema.org

Schema.org is the most important metadata schema in the world of web content. In 2011, the major search engines such as Google and Bing launched schema.org to describe the relationships between entities associated with content. It has fueled the rise of semantic search and knowledge graphs. It has enjoyed wide adoption, and is growing in how it is used.

Google uses content described with schema.org to present its search results (see `Figure 7.1`). For example, customer rating data, when encoded in schema.org, can be displayed in Google's "rich snippets" and "rich cards."

Figure 7.1

Google Search Results Drawing on schema.org Metadata

Nikon D5300 DSLR Camera (Body Only, Black) 1519 B&H Photo Video
https://www.bhphotovideo.com/c/.../nikon_1519_d5300_dslr_camera_black.html ▼
★★★★⯪ Rating: 4.5 - 137 reviews - US$ 596.95
Buy **Nikon D5300** DSLR Camera (Body Only, Black) features 24.2MP DX-Format CMOS Sensor, EXPEED 4 Image Processor. Review Nikon DSLR Cameras, ...

Camera Format: DX / (1.5x Crop Factor)   **Sensor Type / Size**: CMOS, 23.5 x 15.6 mm
Lens Mount: Nikon F   **File Formats**: Still Images: JPEG, RAW; Movies: ...

People who work with web content may be confused about the relationship between schema.org and metadata schemas generally. It's important to remember that schema.org is just one of many metadata schemas that are available. When referring to it, it should always include the domain suffix of "dot-org" to distinguish it from schemas generically. The naming of schema.org was a branding move, designed to create the impression that schema.org was the one schema you needed. However brilliant schema.org's branding, one shouldn't conclude that only schema.org matters.

Schema.org is extremely important for web content, but does not address all metadata requirements for web content. Let's consider how schema.org is different from other schemas.

Terminology. The Schema.org tends to use specific terminology. SEO community, who are the main users of schema.org, rarely refer to schema.org as a kind of metadata. They refer to schema.org as a "vocabulary" for "structured data". Schema.org's terminology is sometimes difficult to integrate into broader discussions of metadata requirements. Other metadata schemas and approaches may use alternate terminology that is sometimes similar sounding, but different in meaning.[110]

Search engine orientation. Schema.org is strongly identified with the fields of search engine optimization and search engine marketing. If metadata requirements are focused exclusively on what schema.org structured data is needed by search engines, insufficient emphasis will be given to other kinds of metadata, such as rights and permissions metadata and technical metadata that rely on other metadata schemas.

Treating structured data for SEO as something separate from other forms of metadata can result in a siloed approach. Web teams working on metadata requirements should aim to bridge the peculiarities of schema.org, with the peculiarities of other metadata schemas. Some of these differences are essentially optical, more about form than about substance. But if not recognized and understood, these differences can hinder developing comprehensive metadata requirements.

Schema.org's outsized influence can dominate metadata discussions, but must also be acknowledged that schema.org is evolving rapidly, expanding into new areas, and it has earned a reputation as the single most important metadata schema for web content.[111]

Goals and Uses

Schema.org is an approach to standardize the semantic description of a wide range of content entities, while providing choices regarding the format used for the metadata description. It currently supports three syntaxes (microdata, RDFa, and JSON-LD) in an effort to appeal to the preferences of different publishers and developers using the data structure.

One basic goal is to structure the data so that it can be displayed outside the context of the content where it is mentioned: for example, as snippets displayed in search results.

Another goal of schema.org is to offer a "single schema across a wide range of topics that included people, places, events, products, offers, and so on."[112] Schema.org is far more comprehensive than either Open Graph or microformats, other options commonly used to add metadata to web content.

Schema.org aims to be a general-purpose data structure than not only describes web content, but supports interactive applications using the information encoded in the metadata. For example, markup about a concert might be used to enable someone to buy a ticket for that a specific performance.

Publishers are largely motivated to use schema.org to enhance how their content appears to search engines. Over time publishers will likely become more interested in using schema.org to support actions that customers want to take within apps on mobile devices, as these capabilities evolve.

Basic Form

Schema.org provides terms to describe types of entities, and properties for entities. You can optionally specify a *resource* (the subject of the content described) that formally identifies who or what is being described. Otherwise, the resource may be described anonymously (from a machine point of view), where the subject of the encoded metadata description not linked to other metadata descriptions elsewhere about the same resource.[113] The metadata might include properties about a subject named "John Johnson", but it will not make clear which John Johnson is being described unless that resource is linked to a unambiguous reference, such as a reference to a specific Wikipedia article about a particular John Johnson.[114]

The creators of schema.org decided not to require publishers to explicitly identify a resource (i.e., an entity described in the content) with a link to other references to that entity elsewhere. They decided that making publishers coordinate references to an entity with references about it on other websites using hyperlinks, was too big a burden for many publishers. "Unfortunately, coordinating entity references with other sites for the tens of thousands of entities about which a site may have information is much too difficult for most sites."[115] Search engines use the attributes and values to infer what entity is being described, using a knowledge base.

Indicating only the attributes and values reduces the effort to encode the metadata, though it can limit some broader applications of the markup outside of supporting search results.

Specifying Details

Schema.org allows authors to include as much or as little detail as they want. Descriptions can be statements, or references to descriptions made elsewhere, which may be extensive. In principle, authors only need to make statements for values when they aren't already expressed elsewhere, provided they include a valid link to the metadata containing that information. The ability to reuse one's own and other organizations' metadata embodies the goal of "don't repeat yourself."

Another feature of schema.org is that two different types of entities can be linked together, where the relationship between them is made explicit. The subject being described may have an attribute whose value is another entity. For example, schema.org might indicate an Organization has a founder who is a Person.

Broad organization

Coverage

Currently, schema.org covers the following categories of entities:

- Action
- CreativeWork
- Event
- Intangible
- MedicalEntity
- Organization
- Person
- Place
- Product

Most of these categories (with the exception of Person) are broken into more specific entity types (see `Figure 7.2`).

Figure 7.2

The Breadth of Entity Types Available in schema.org

Actions	Creative Works	Intangibles	MedicalEntity
AchieveAction	Article	AlignmentObject	AnatomicalStructure
AssessAction	Blog	Audience	AnatomicalSystem
ConsumeAction	Book	Brand	MedicalCause
ControlAction	Clip	BroadcastChannel	MedicalCondition
CreateAction	Code	BusTrip	MedicalContraindication
FindAction	Comment	Class	MedicalDevice
InteractAction	CreativeWorkSeason	DataFeedItem	MedicalGuideline
MoveAction	CreativeWorkSeries	Demand	MedicalIndication
OrganizeAction	DataCatalog	EntryPoint	MedicalIntangible
PlayAction	Dataset	Enumeration	MedicalProcedure
SearchAction	Diet	Flight	MedicalRiskEstimator
TradeAction	EmailMessage	GameServer	MedicalRiskFactor
TransferAction	Episode	Invoice	MedicalSignOrSymptom
UpdateAction	ExercisePlan	ItemList	MedicalStudy
	Game	JobPosting	MedicalTest
Events	Map	Language	MedicalTherapy
BusinessEvent	MediaObject	ListItem	SuperficialAnatomy
ChildrensEvent	Movie	Offer	
ComedyEvent	MusicComposition	Order	**Organizations**
DanceEvent	MusicPlaylist	OrderItem	Airline
DeliveryEvent	MusicRecording	ParcelDelivery	Corporation
EducationEvent	Painting	Permit	EducationalOrganization
ExhibitionEvent	Photograph	ProgramMembership	GovernmentOrganization
Festival	PublicationIssue	Property	LocalBusiness
FoodEvent	PublicationVolume	PropertyValueSpecification	NGO
LiteraryEvent	Question	Quantity	PerformingGroup
MusicEvent	Recipe	Rating	SportsOrganization
PublicationEvent	Review	Reservation	
SaleEvent	Sculpture	Role	**Persons**
ScreeningEvent	Season	Seat	
SocialEvent	Series	Service	**Places**
SportsEvent	SoftwareApplication	ServiceChannel	AdministrativeArea
TheaterEvent	SoftwareSourceCode	StructuredValue	CivicStructure
UserInteraction	TVSeason	Ticket	Landform
VisualArtsEvent	TVSeries	TrainTrip	LandmarksOrHistoricalBuildings
	VisualArtwork		LocalBusiness
	WebPage	**Products**	Residence
	WebPageElement	IndividualProduct	TouristAttraction
	WebSite	ProductModel	
		SomeProducts	
		Vehicle	

Entity Hierarchy

Entity types are organized hierarchically (see Figure 7.3). An entity type can be broken into more specific entity types, which inherit all the properties of its parent, and will have unique properties of its own. The hierarchy can continue for more than one level. A Creative Work includes over three-dozen sub-entities, such as Article and Game. The Article entity has more specific entities such as News Article and Report.

Figure 7.3
Schema.org Entity Hierarchy

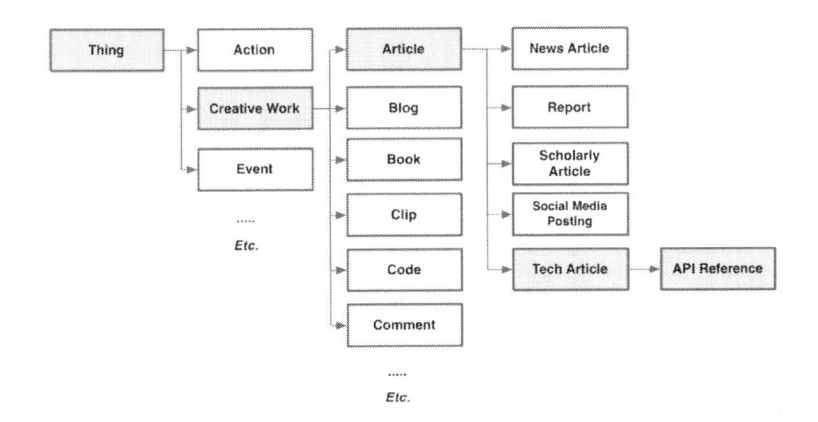

```
Thing ──► Action          Article ────► News Article
       ├─► Creative Work ─► Blog   ────► Report
       │   Event          ─► Book  ────► Scholarly Article
       │   .....          ─► Clip  ────► Social Media Posting
       │   Etc.           ─► Code  ────► Tech Article ──► API Reference
       │                  ─► Comment
       │                     .....
       │                     Etc.
```

Publishers generally will identify entities by the entity type that is most specific to what is being described. Using a specific entity type allows the use of properties that are specific to the entity, in addition to properties associated with more general entities higher up in the hierarchy.

Properties

Entity types have a range of properties, both those specific to the entity type, as well as those inherited from more general entity types higher in the hierarchy. For example, all entities are children of the parent entity called **Thing**. The Thing entity contains some generic properties, such as name, description, and URL, that can be used to describe any entity.

An entity can be described using any property associated with its entity type or its parent. Many properties allow an entity to refer to another type of entity. An **Event** might indicate its location by declaring a **Place** entity type, and then provide the address using **Postal Address** entity type, for example.

Properties have an *expected type*, which is either an entity type (for cases with compound values are required), or a simple value corresponding to a recognized data type:

- `Boolean`
- `Date`
- `DateTime`
- `Number`
- `Text`
- `Time`.

Schema.org specifies what entity types can be used as values for properties. Most often only publishers are allowed to use one specific entity type only. But for some properties, publishers have a choice what entity type to use as a value: for example, whether the list the author as a person or as an organization.

Schema.org has special intangible entity type called `Enumeration`. Enumerations are used to specify text values for common situations in standardized ways. Various subtypes of `Enumeration` exist, often addressing the status or variant of common entities. For example, events have an `EventStatusType`, which has enumerations covering four values: `EventCancelled`, `EventPostponed`, `EventRescheduled`, and `EventScheduled`.

A key dilemma when using schema.org is deciding what properties need to be included. Schema.org itself does not make the inclusion of any properties in a description as mandatory. It is up to both the creators of the metadata, and the consumers of metadata, to make those decisions themselves. For example, Google provides guidance on what fields to include that will display in rich snippets. It provides validation tools that offer recommendations on properties to use. For example, if the content describes a product that is for sale, Google requires that the price be presented, even though this is not a requirement of the schema.org schema. Google-specific guidance relating to required and recommended properties may not be followed in the same way by other search engines. Moreover, search engines are only one potential application of schema.org metadata, even if they are the dominant one. Content publishers may decide to mandate the inclusion of certain properties within their own content systems, to ensure these details are always captured.

Example

In `Chapter 6`, we encountered some code examples featuring the schema.org data structure, which can be written using either microdata, RDFa or JSON-LD. Let's look at a more conceptual example to focus on how schema.org descriptions work.

Figure 7.4 provides a visual representation of how schema.org identifies dimensions of a `CreativeWork`, an entity type that covers things from recipes to movies to software applications.[116] It illustrates how a `CreativeWork` entity would reference other entity types, such as `Person` and `Organization`. Most of the properties of a `CreativeWork` are self-explanatory: a name (possibly the title of the work), a description, an author, a publisher, and a date published. The one property that might not be self-explanatory is `about`, which refers to subject matter of the content. It is a plain text field, meaning that any kind of verbal description is allowed.

Figure 7.4

A Diagram Shows Metadata Describing a Creativework Using Schema.Org.[117]

(CC-by courtesy of Phil Barker and Lorna M. Campbell)

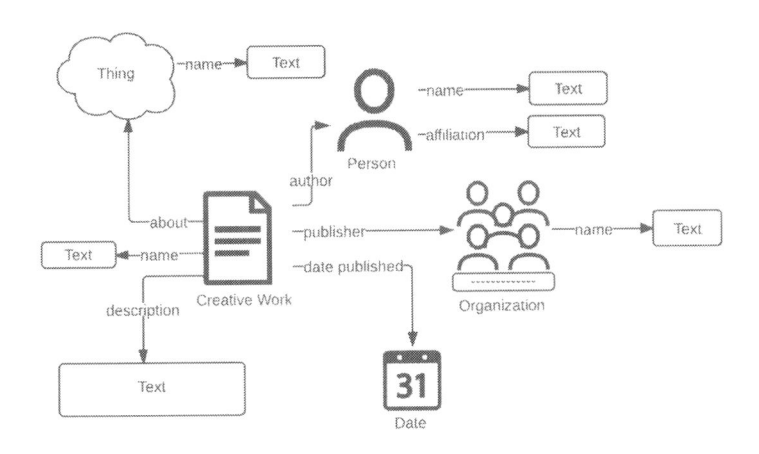

While entity types indicate the properties that can be used to describe an entity, the entity type does not mandate that a property be included. The example illustrates the kinds of properties that *could* be included, but some of these might not be, and in fact there are many other properties associated with the creative work entity type that are not present in this example. Schema.org has a permissive data structure that does not require that certain attributes be mandatory.[118] We will discuss this matter further shortly.

Issues and Limitations

Schema.org is an ambitious undertaking, and is continually evolving. Although it is becoming increasingly comprehensive, and documentation relating to it is becoming more extensive, it is sometimes not self-evident what is the correct or best way to implement schema.org. Fortunately an active online community exists to address these issues, which often feeds into future enhancements of schema.org.

Choosing Correct Entity Types. It's not always clear which entity type to choose when describing an entity. Sometimes two entity types seem similar. Many writers wonder whether to choose `Article` or `BlogPosting` as the entity type.

Explicit guidance on the precise boundaries of an entity is sometimes limited, and must be inferred based on the properties available. In the case of `Article` and `BlogPosting`, many of the properties are similar. In such a case, people have the option to declare alternative entity types to describe sort of entity.

Another kind of issue arises when describing a more complex concept that has a range of properties. Although entities are normally associated with a single entity type, some entities are *multi-type entities* that declare more than one entity type in order to use the properties relating to those types.

Selecting the most appropriate entity type depends on two issues. First, some entity types include certain properties that other entity types don't include. The choice of entity type will depend partly on which properties and values belonging to the metadata description are most important to emphasize. Second, when two or more options are available, one might be preferable because it is more commonly used or supported. Google, for example, presents structured data for certain entity types as rich snippets, but not for other types.

Coverage Gaps. Initially, schema.org was created to address the needs of online marketers. While the coverage has expanded over time, it is still largely oriented to the needs of firms that sell products and services. There can be gaps in entities and properties available to provide a full description of content that is not commercially oriented. For example, at least as of the time of this writing, schema.org has a very limited range of properties relating to religious topics.

The creators of schema.org have characterized the evolution of the data structure as one of "incremental complexity."[119] The structure will become richer over time, with additional properties and subtypes, some additional capabilities such as new types of actions and events, and additional domains that will broaden the range of entities that can be described in detail. One important initiative has been the development of *extensions* to schema.org to address more specialized domains, such as medical, automotive and bibliographic terminology.

Dublin Core

Dublin Core was the first metadata schema created to describe internet content, and it can be used to describe physical media such as catalogs as well.[120] The virtue of Dublin Core is that it can be used to describe most anything, though not necessarily at a high level of detail.

Goals and uses

The motivation behind Dublin Core is to offer a simple and widely applicable data structure. Because it is lightweight, flexible and easy to understand, Dublin Core can be used in a variety of situations to clarify the meaning of content.

Dublin Core has a unique position in the field of metadata schemas. It is used primarily to *manage* certain kinds of digital content, but it is not widely used to *publish* web content. Dublin Core metadata sometimes appears in the head of an HTML document, within the `<meta>` element. But overall Dublin Core isn't widely used in published web content, and web search engines do not seem to utilize Dublin Core metadata.

Dublin Core most often used to support internal content management requirements. For example, it is used by a wide range of institutions that manage digital content, from museums to photo repositories. Publishers often acquire content from external sources that uses Dublin Core markup. Dublin Core metadata is used in many digital asset management systems to describe photos and other media assets that are published.

Another reason to be familiar with Dublin Core is that is utilized by some other important metadata standards. It has also influenced the development of standards.

Although stature of Dublin Core is waning, it is still important to know about, because of its indirect influence on content systems and on other schemas.

Broad organization

Dublin Core has 15 core **elements**, covering:

- Administrative dimensions (`Creator, Publisher, Date, Identifier, Source, Language`)
- Descriptive dimensions (`Title, Subject, Description, Type, Relation, Coverage`)
- Technical dimensions (`Format`)
- Rights dimensions (`Rights`).

The core elements are supplemented by over 50 **terms** that can describe the elements in more granular detail, or address additional aspects. For example, the coverage of content can be described in terms of temporal coverage and spatial coverage. Dublin Core also provides **types** to indicate content type or format. `Figure 7.5` shows the Dublin Core elements, terms, and types.

Figure 7.5.
Dublin Core Metadata Descriptors

Dublin Core

Elements	*Terms*	*Types*
Contributor Coverage Creator Date Description Format Identifier Language Publisher Relation Rights Source Subject Title Type	abstract, accessRights, accrualMethod, accrualPeriodicity, accrualPolicy, alternative, audience, available, bibliographicCitation, conformsTo, contributor, coverage, created, creator, date, dateAccepted, dateCopyrighted, dateSubmitted, description, educationLevel, extent, format, hasFormat, hasPart, hasVersion, identifier, instructionalMethod, isFormatOf, isPartOf, isReferencedBy, isReplacedBy, isRequiredBy, issued, isVersionOf, language, license, mediator, medium, modified, provenance, publisher, references, relation, replaces, requires, rights, rightsHolder, source, spatial, subject, tableOfContents, temporal, title, type, valid	Collection Dataset Event Image InteractiveResource MovingImage PhysicalObject Service Software Sound StillImage Text

Example

To indicate the language of content, Dublin Core can use the language element, which is "dc.language". The value of the language can be encoded in a machine readable format, in this case by using "en" to indicate English.

```
<!DOCTYPE html>
<html>
```

```
<head>  ❶
    <meta charset="utf-8">
    <title>Title in English</title>
    <meta name="dc.language" content="en">  ❷
</head>
<body>
</body>
</html>
```

❶ In this example, the Dublin Core metadata is placed within the HTML <head>.

❷ Dublin Core elements can be indicated in HTML as with the name attribute followed by the Dublin Core element name. This example illustrates the use of a machine-readable value.

Dublin Core has influenced newer metadata schemas, including the Open Graph protocol.

Open Graph Protocol

Facebook created a metadata schema called the Open Graph protocol (OGP).[121] The Open Graph protocol overlaps with schema.org in coverage, but is generally less detailed, and covers a narrower range of items. It is a lightweight metadata schema oriented toward the needs of social networking platforms to support social graphs, which represent a person's relationships with both people and things.

The Open Graph protocol refers to content items as "objects." In the words of the OGP website: "The Open Graph protocol enables any web page to become a rich object in a social graph. For instance, this is used on Facebook to allow any web page to have the same functionality as any other object on Facebook."[122] In practice that means a web page marked up with Open Graph looks and acts like other items people interact with on Facebook, such as posts and videos by Facebook users.

Goals and uses

Open Graph supports content discovery, and enables software apps to interact with content items.

1. **Discovery**

Open Graph markup influences how content is displayed on social media platforms. It may influence what content is seen by whom, though how is done in practice is subject to variation. Content publishers can obtain behavioral analytics relating to their content if they have commercial relationship with a social media platform that entitles them to this data.

2. **Actions on Objects**

Facebook uses Open Graph to learn what its members are "liking." Facebook can associate actions with objects described with the Open Graph protocol.[123] Different entity types can be associated with different action types. A restaurant can be visited, and a video may be watched, or noted as `wants_to_watch`.

Broad Organization

1. **Core Elements**

Open Graph core elements include:

- Standard descriptive metadata such as title and description

- Administrative metadata concerning author, publisher, contact information, ID, content source (site name, canonical URL)

- Rights metadata relating to locale and locale restrictions, and age restrictions.

2. **Object-Specific Elements**

Specific entity types have object-specific metadata. Objects include:

- Article
- Books
- Business
- Fitness
- Game
- Music
- Place
- Product
- Profile (Person)
- Restaurant
- Video.

A restaurant, for example, includes elements for category and price range, in addition to core elements to specify location.

Open Graph Example

Pinterest markup is known as Rich Pins. For some kinds of Pins such as articles, products and places, it uses metadata described in Open Graph (as well as from schema.org) to get information about the item displayed.

The following Pinterest metadata for a product uses various Open Graph elements.[124]. An interesting characteristic of Open Graph metadata is that the values are invisible when content is viewed as a standard web page, but will be visible to audiences when accessed through an application that reads Open Graph metadata.

```
<head>  ❶
<meta property="og:type" content="product" />❷
<meta property="og:title" content="Technology Will Save Us Gamer DIY Kit" />
<meta property="og:description" content="One of the permanent installations in the collection of Humble Masterpieces at the Museum of Modern Art in New York, this DIY gamer kit from London-based company Technology Will Save Us is equal parts gadget and design classic. " />  ❸
<meta property="og:url" content="http://www.urbanoutfitters.com/...75900 />
<meta property="og:site_name" content="Urban Outfitters" />
```

```
<meta property="og:price:amount"
content="98.00" />
<meta property="og:price:currency"
content="USD" />
<meta property="og:availability"
content="instock" />
</head>
```

❶ The metadata is contained within the HTML `<head>` element.

❷ The attributes of the description are announced by the phrase `property`, and the values will commonly be announced by the phrase `content`. In this example, the metadata is indicating that the description refers to a product entity.

❸ In this example, the description that is meant for people accessing an application such as Pinterest that uses Open Graph metadata.

Popular Specialized Schemas

There are numerous specialized metadata schemas that are targeted for a specific purpose. The following are among the more widely used or widely applicable.

- **FOAF**

Friend of a Friend (FOAF) is a well-established semantic metadata schema to describe people and their relationships with other people.[125] It is similar in coverage to the `h-card` microformat for contact information, but it includes a richer set of attributes covering relationships people may have with others, such as employment, social and family relationships. It is often used to identify authors of digital content, by listing their affiliations and their digital identities such websites and social media profiles, so that people can distinguish between persons who might have the same name, or link together a person who might use different variants of their name.

- **GoodRelations**

GoodRelations is an ecommerce schema adopted by a number of large retailers to describe their products online. It indicates the agent (organization selling), an object (a product or service for sale), the offer, and location. Its "conceptual model" has been absorbed by schema.org, but coexists as a separate approach to defining product attributes.[126] Despite overlap between GoodRelations and schema.org, GoodRelations may offer additional granularity for some entity types that can be used to extend what's available in Schema.org.

- **Open Annotation**

Open Annotations is a W3C standard to permit interoperable annotation of content, whether text, images or video.[127] It can be used to support commenting and discussions about articles or other comment, or to elicit crowdsourced knowledge about an item, for example, identifying people or things in a photograph.

- **XMP**

XMP (Extensible Metadata Platform) uses XML to express both descriptive and technical metadata about photos. Created by Adobe, it is now an ISO standard, supported by photo viewing and editing applications, and digital asset management systems.[128] XMP is used by some applications to allow people to tag the faces of people appearing in photos.

Proprietary Schemas

While all the data structures discussed thus far have been open standards that are intended to be used by anyone, some proprietary metadata schemas are important to know about as well. Certain content distribution platforms ask publishers to add specialized tags to their content so that the platform can use the metadata for its own purposes.

- **Twitter Cards**

Twitter accepts some Open Graph markup, but has a few specialized tags that affect how content is referenced and displayed within Twitter. These attributes are placed within the HTML `<meta>` element and use the prefix `twitter:`.[129]

- **Facebook Instant Articles**

Facebook has introduced a publishing program called instant articles. While the markup guidelines largely rely on HTML5 standards, Facebook as introduced some proprietary attributes (signified by the prefix op :) for use within HTML elements.[130]

---

[110] There are numerous metadata schemas that do not use the term *structured data*, but instead use the terms *metadata* and *schemas*. Google and its schema.org partners did not follow these conventions. Google is the most active evangelist for schema.org. Google's help pages for webmasters have been influential in framing the discussion of metadata. These help pages refer to structured data, rather than to metadata.

[111] Increasingly, as schema.org evolves, it is allowing the use of metadata defined by other schemas.

[112] R.V. Guha, Dan Brickley, and Steve Macbeth, "Schema.org: Evolution of Structured Data on the Web" *ACM Queue* December 15, 2015

[113] This can be a difficult concept to understand. Imagine you have pages on two web sites both talking about "ABC Corp." One page says ABC's location is New York. Another page says ABC's location is Chicago. Are these pages talking about the same ABC Corp.? Search engines such as Google may be able to infer that they are two locations of the same company, even though the mentions of the companies on the two pages aren't directly or indirectly linked together. But it is also possible that Google can't make that inference, and assumes that two companies named ABC exist, based in different locations. Without linking the resource specified, there is the possibility that the resource will not be correctly identified by search engines.

[114] Wikipedia is a good example of why disambiguation is important. The names of the things discussed in many Wikipedia articles are similar or identical. The linking to Wikipedia identifiers will be discussed in Chapter 8.

[115] Guha, Brickley and Macbeth, *Ibid*.

[116] In schema.org syntax, entities are written in upper CamelCase.

[117] Image CC-By license from Phil Barker and Lorna M. Campbell, "What is Schema.org?" *Centre for Educational Technology, Interoperability and Standards*. June 2014. http://publications.cetis.org.uk/2014/960

[118] For those interested, a clarification of how I am using certain words. I may say that properties *define* an entity type, because they provide a comprehensive listing of attributes that can be used to characterize an entity, and only those attributes can be used, as they alone are permitted by the entity type definition. In contrast, I may say that specific properties *describe* an instance of an entity, since there is no expectation that the properties included in the metadata description of a specific entity instance are comprehensive and complete, and they therefore only partially describe the entity, rather than define it unambiguously.

[119] Guha, Brickley and Macbeth, *Ibid*.

[120] The Dublin Core website, http://dublincore.org, states: "The Dublin Core Metadata Initiative (DCMI) is an open organization managed as a project of ASIS&T" (the Association for Information Science and Technology, a nonprofit membership organization).

[121] According to the OGP website: "The Open Graph protocol was originally created at Facebook and is inspired by Dublin Core, link-rel canonical, Microformats, and RDFa." see http://ogp.me

[122] *ibid*.

[123] Facebook actions: https://developers.facebook.com/docs/reference/opengraph

[124] "Product Pins" Pinterest https://developers.pinterest.com/docs/rich-pins/products/

[125] "FOAF Vocabulary Specification",
`http://xmlns.com/foaf/spec/`
[126] "GoodRelations and schema.org" *GoodRelations website*,
`http://wiki.goodrelations-vocabulary.org/GoodRelations_and_schema.org`
[127] Open Annotation Model,
`http://www.openannotation.org/spec/core/`
[128] "Extensible Metadata Platform (XMP)",
`http://www.adobe.com/products/xmp.html`
[129] "Cards Markup Tag Reference"
`https://dev.twitter.com/cards/markup`
[130] "Instant Articles Format Reference"
`https://developers.facebook.com/docs/instant-articles/reference`

Choosing a Schema

With many data standards available, publishers need to choose which standard to use. A range of options exist, depending on one's needs. The general advice is to choose the simplest option that can achieve the goals of the organization.

1. **Adopt a Single Standard**

The simplest option is to use one specific standard. Many businesses that are active in ecommerce can use schema.org without needing other schemas. Such an approach reduces the complexity of markup, but may limit exposure in social media channels. So while it can be helpful to rely on one standard as the primary basis for marking up content, it is often advisable to supplement the markup with other standards that offer additional capabilities.

2. **Mix Multiple Standards**

Most often, a combination of two or more data structure standards will offer the range of description that organizations need. For example, many publishers need to ensure exposure of web content on both the Google search and Facebook social media platforms, and therefore add both schema.org and Open Graph metadata to their content.

Combining and mixing standards is possible by declaring the namespaces of all the schemas being used. Using more than one standard does add complexity, but this can be managed if each schema plays a specific role, and the content system is designed so that the appropriate schema is used for the particular role required.

3. Extend a Standard

In some cases, a schema may be nearly sufficient for one's purposes, but it doesn't offer sufficient detail in some critical area. A standard can be extended using the same syntax as the source standard. This may be an option when an organization needed to describe specialized entities. It is possible to share an extension with the public, so that other organizations can also use the extension. Schema.org allows outside parties to develop and host extensions that would be of broad interest.[131]

4. Create Custom Schema

Organizations can develop and publish their own schemas, effectively creating new data standards. This is generally only done by very large organizations with specialized needs, and who are in a position to impose their standards on their suppliers and business partners. For example, Amazon has specific data requirements for firms wanting to list products on its platform.[132] Certain government agencies and international organizations may also be in a position to unilaterally create a schema and expect that others will use it.

Often, proprietary custom schemas later become open standards to encourage wider adoption. The transformation of Adobe's custom XMP schema into an open standard is an example of this.

[131] "Schema.org Extensions",
https://schema.org/docs/extension.html

[132] Amazon Services, "Selling on Amazon Guide to XML",
https://images-na.ssl-images-amazon.com/images/G/01/rainier/help/XML_Documentation_Intl.pdf

Chapter 8. Data Values & Controlled Vocabularies

CHAPTER PREVIEW

Data values refer to the values associated with metadata attributes. They play an important role in how IT systems interpret metadata, and the ability of these systems to act on the metadata to manage, assemble and deliver content. Most values in web content metadata are text. **Controlled vocabularies** provide a list of what terms can be used as text values in metadata. Often, controlled vocabularies will indicate the relationship of different terms to one another, within a hierarchical taxonomy. Controlled vocabularies can make metadata easier to enter, and they bring consistency to how attributes are described, improving the quality and reliability of the metadata as a result.

Since web content may discuss many topics, metadata relating to it can involve many distinct text values. To utilize a controlled vocabulary, publishers have two options. They can use existing controlled vocabularies that have been developed by other organizations such a trade associations. This is frequently the best option, because it requires less effort, the quality of the terminology is generally high, and the terminology is widely used by many organizations.

The second option is to create **taxonomies** to support unique needs. Developing a taxonomy of one's own can involve significant effort and calls for the participation and agreement of many different stakeholders in an organization to ensure all requirements are addressed. The task involves deciding how to categorize and name things that are mentioned in the content.

Different approaches are used to developing one's own taxonomy. One common approach is to look at different **facets** or aspects discussed in the content to identify themes important to the business to include in the taxonomy. Another common activity is to define **broader and narrower relationships** between different terms that will be used in the taxonomy as text values for the metadata.

Getting the Facts Right

Web content involves lots of facts. Some facts are about the content, such as who wrote it, and other facts are embedded within the content, such as what products or companies are mentioned. Data values are a formalization of the facts associated with the content. For data values to deliver value as data that can be used in many contexts by many different people, it's important that everyone involved with publishing and consuming the content knows that the facts are "right" — the facts aren't ambiguous. Different people, and different machines, shouldn't have a difference of opinion about what a fact means.

Data value consistency is a key issue in web content metadata. As discussed in Chapter 3, the values used in metadata descriptions are generally categories, quantities, names, or descriptions.[133] Publishers must decide how much consistency is useful and necessary for these values. When specifying structured data values, they need to consider how important the values will be for different scenarios: exchanging information with partners, aggregating large quantities of content, merging content from different systems, or supporting internationalization and localization, to name a few.

In order to appreciate how IT systems use data values, it helps to distinguish data values that involve words, from those that involve numbers. IT systems treat these values as variables when managing or delivering content.

Data values in web content metadata are most often words — the names of things or qualities of properties — which to computers are *text strings* — sequences of characters.

In addition to words, other kinds of values are used in web content metadata. Sometimes the value of an attribute is an ID number of some kind. ID numbers aren't actually quantities that can be computed, but are a special kind of alphanumeric string. Data values can also be different kinds of numbers: quantities, dates, times, currency values, and geolocation coordinates, among others.[134] These different kinds of data values (word strings, IDs, various numeric values) are known as *data types*.

This chapter will focus data values involving words — the text data type. We will consider numeric values in `Chapter 9`.

The utility of text values used in metadata can be enhanced using *controlled vocabularies*. Controlled vocabularies specify what words or phrases authors should use as metadata attributes. They are an agreed set of rules for words used to describe things. They provide a list of allowed terms that must be used in metadata descriptions. They can also provide clear guidance on which term to use, if several possibilities exist. Controlled vocabularies are most commonly used with text values that are categories or names. They are rarely used with longer verbal descriptions.

When computers see consistent text values, they can take actions based on predictable values. Consistent terminology is a major element influencing metadata quality — another major element, how text and numeric values are formatted, will be discussed in Chapter 9.

Controlled vocabularies complement metadata schemas, but are different from them. Where metadata schemas define the attributes associated with entities, controlled vocabularies define the values that can be used with these attributes. Metadata schemas, such as schema.org, do not provide guidance on what values to use for word-based descriptions.

What something is called can have big consequences. Authors need to understand what a value means, and use it consistently. Suppose the metadata needs to describe how big something is. One author may be inclined to indicate the size attribute as "large". Another author will think the size is "medium". Yet another considers the size is big, and indicates the size as "jumbo." We can see some problems. We don't have an agreed standard for what is big, and what is not big. And we don't have an agreed standard for describing something even when everyone agrees it is big.[135]

If different authors describe an attribute of a product in different ways, the metadata will loose its usefulness. Another simple example is how to describe colors. Should the color of a t-shirt be described as burgundy, as wine, or perhaps as crimson red? Which color is the best one to use? If two values seem similar, how does one know which is the correct one to use?

Controlled vocabularies can take the form of a *taxonomy* (a hierarchical controlled vocabulary containing broader and narrower terms), as a *thesaurus* (a taxonomy indicating what non-preferred terms are equivalent to preferred ones), or as an *ontology* (a classification system for representing concepts, which groups items together based on common properties they share.) Taxonomies are the most common kind of controlled vocabulary.[136]

In short, controlled vocabularies are useful for two reasons. First, they improve the *usability* of metadata for those needing to enter it. Second, they improve the *reliability* of the metadata for IT systems, by improving the quality of what is described by metadata.

---

[133] A fifth kind of value, IDs, can be thought of as a special kind of description, and will be addressed later in this chapter.
[134] Data formats provide guidance for many non-text values, as will be discussed in Chapter 9.

[135] Some might argue that using a single word to indicate size is too vague, and they'd be right to a point. A single word can stand for a more complex idea such as dimensions and weight that would involve more attributes and more precision. In some situations, metadata needs to offer a summary value that describes an item — for example, so that audiences can make high level choices before drilling into details.

[136] Controlled vocabularies can take many forms, and have various features. Historically information professionals have emphasized differences in the types of controlled vocabularies in use, but more modern controlled vocabularies have started to include features from previously distinct approaches. I will discuss taxonomies in particular because they are a core concept in controlled vocabularies. Not all controlled vocabularies are based on a hierarchical taxonomy, but more complex ones generally do.

Ensuring Consistency in Descriptions

Web content metadata is a team effort, and in no area is this more important than making sure all stakeholders agree to what the metadata means. It is common in organizations for different departments to use slightly different terminology to refer to similar things. Such a practice may be annoying in an inter-office email, but it can be crippling for metadata, because different groups of people may be entering different words or phrases to represent certain values. Sometimes the differences seem subtle, such as when a full and abbreviated term both exist with metadata descriptions. But to IT systems, these differences weaken how valuable the metadata is.

Everyone involved with describing content needs to agree on the form of a description, and buy into the process for agreeing to it. Since buy-in is critical, it is useful to know the range of approaches available, to understand the strengths and weaknesses of each.

Developing effective, consistent descriptions is not a trivial task. Data values need to be clear to everyone *and* precise for IT systems. Sometimes those goals are compatible, but other times they can be in conflict with each other.

Common Approaches to Text Values

Publishers use text values to represent a name or a category for an attribute in web content. Text values are subject to differing interpretations. For everyone to describe things consistently, they need a shared mental model of what the description represents. That is, everyone needs to have a common understanding of what the value represents.

Let's consider three kinds of text values that publishers commonly use:

1. Global IDs
2. Feature-based Descriptions
3. Plain Language Descriptions

Each has strengths and weaknesses. Controlled vocabularies, taxonomies in particular, are important tools to manage potential problems with these approaches.

Global IDs

Many organizations use global unique identifiers (GUIDs) to identify specific entities. GUIDs are strings that aren't words. The fact that the string has no intrinsic meaning is its major weakness.

A unique ID is like a serial number on a valuable item, in contrast to a reusable ID such as part number covering many pieces of identical parts. GUIDs are a string of letters and numbers that represent an entity being described. A customer number would be an example of this. They have the benefit of disambiguating two terms that might be identical or seem very similar. Two customers may both be named Joe Bloggs, but each has a separate customer ID, so they aren't confused.

While GUIDs help prevent similar-sounding concepts from being confused, they aren't very meaningful to humans. GUIDs are opaque. And GUIDs, while precise, can sometimes make false distinctions. It might turn out that two GUIDs referring to someone with the same name is actually just one person. A second identity got created because the original identity wasn't available or seen, which may happen if information is being handled by separate systems that aren't integrated. Such issues are common, especially when the identifier doesn't mean much conceptually to be person creating it. Such duplication requires what is called *entity resolution*: determining what entities are in fact refer to the same thing. Because GUIDs have no meaning by themselves, entities must rely on other identifying attributes to make clear what is being identified with certainty.

Feature-based Descriptions as Identifiers

Some identifiers are generated from logical components. Feature-based descriptions follow this pattern. An article of clothing might be described according to a formula: **gender + color + brand + garment type**. The garment is described as a man's red H&M t-shirt or a woman's blue Zara t-shirt. Such phrasal descriptions are meaningful to humans, who can readily understand what the identifier refers to. But such descriptions are less useful as metadata identifiers, because much valuable information is jammed together. An identifying phrase composed of features is trying to do two things at once. Instead of simply identifying something, the phrase is also trying to describe it.

Feature-based descriptions offer low precision. It can be hard to see duplicate items when using a description based on features. They can require care to use effectively. They are sometimes brittle, unable to accommodate new descriptive requirements easily. You may later need to include the type of fabric to distinguish different t-shirts. Or you may want to re-categorize a man's t-shit as unisex. Using a single description to identify something uniquely is generally not a good idea.

Plain Language Descriptions

Rather than identify an entity with a single encoded value such as a GUID or feature-based description, an entity can be described using multiple attributes – as many as are required to describe the characteristics that are important. The combination of attributes allows entities to be identified, as well as indicate how they differ from related entities.

Each attribute is described by a separate word or phrase. Rather than use an artificial ID or terminology construct, the description uses plain language. Although a single word or phrase addressing an single attribute will generally not uniquely identify the content, when used in combination to describe different attributes of the content, the values can offer both clarity and precision.

These verbal descriptions are easy for authors and readers to understand. But words within metadata descriptions can sometimes be difficult for computers to interpret. For example, an abstract for an article can identify the subject matter of the article for readers, but won't help computers track and manage the topic.

To use plain language in text values, authors need guidelines for making word choices. Controlled vocabularies and taxonomies provide such guidelines. They prevent people from making descriptions that are inconsistent with the preferred standard.

A Hybrid Word-ID Approach

The above approaches are not mutually exclusive. Some publishers employ a hybrid approach combining plain language and IDs to represent the values for attributes.

Consider how to represent the value of a color. A publisher could maintain separate fields for an color ID number and for a color text description, which are used in combination to describe the attribute. This approach involves more work, but can be more flexible. If the color term is accompanied by a unique ID, that allows the term to change in the future. While most organizations will want to use terminology that is consistent over time, under some circumstances they may want to change the terms they use. A firm may want to stop referring to the color as wine, and start referring to it as burgundy. If there is an ID associated with those color names, terms can change while maintaining continuity.

How to Develop Common Terminology

Publishers need a reliable process to develop common terminology to describe values in metadata attributes.

Controlled vocabularies can evolve through either a centralized or decentralized process. Centralized processes generate more reliable consistency, provided all parties agree to the standards set.

Top Down, or Centralized Processes

Most controlled vocabularies are planned. A central coordinating committee or working group, such as a trade association or standards body, assumes responsibility for defining controlled vocabularies. Committees may meet on a scheduled basis, and release numbered versions of a controlled vocabulary. Examples of organizations that develop controlled vocabulary standards are **GS1**, a global organization dedicated to commerce standards, and **IPTC**, a international body of news organizations.[137] These vocabularies are intentionally designed, actively governed and are generally stable. Compliance with top down standards is generally clear-cut: either one complies, or doesn't.

Centralized, top-down approaches work best when buy-in is likely, because the parties that need to follow the vocabulary belong to the same organization, and are therefore aligned around goals that the vocabulary supports.

Bottom Up, or Decentralized Processes

Decentralized processes rely on norms, conventions, and incremental additions and modifications to established practices.

The example of **Wikipedia** illustrates a decentralized process to a controlled vocabulary. Many publishers rely on Wikipedia to provide their controlled vocabulary — if the term has an entry in Wikipedia, then it is allowed as a term in the publisher's metadata. With Wikipedia, anyone can propose additions or changes to entity entries. Wikipedia provides a process and set of criteria that determines what is allowed.

Decentralized processes can be flexible, but represent a lesser degree of consensus. It is possible that inconsistencies in the vocabulary can be introduced using a decentralized approach. The vocabulary may be subject to change at any time, which can occasionally complicate the implementation and general maintenance of metadata incorporating entities used in Wikipedia, as will be discussed shortly.

The example of **microformats** illustrates another variation of a bottom-up approach, where conventions in use are repurposed to create an open source resource that people can voluntarily follow. Because there is no formal standard, but a recommended practice, the consistency achieved depends on the extent that parties choose to adopt the practice.

Bottom-up approaches are used when buy-in is more difficult, because the parties don't belong to a common organization. One bottom-up tactic is to leverage commonly used terms that aren't fully standardized, and recommend a standard form for these terms. The United Nations has adopted this approach to communicate about disaster relief on Twitter. They utilize Twitter hashtags, and provide recommended structure for terms. For example, when discussing Ebola, they encourage the use of tags such as **#EbolaSL** for discussion of the Ebola outbreak in Sierra Leone, and **#EbolaNeed** for discussion of what is needed relating to the outbreak.[138]

---

[137] GS1 has developed the "GS1 Web Vocabulary", see http://www.gs1.org/voc/ . IPTC has developed "Media Topics", see http://cv.iptc.org/newscodes/mediatopic

[138] United Nations Office for the Coordination of Humanitarian Affairs, "Hashtag Standards for Emergencies", October 2014, http://reliefweb.int/sites/reliefweb.int/files/resources/Hashtag%20Standards%20For%20Emergencies.pdf

Using External Controlled Vocabularies

Many kinds of controlled vocabularies have been created, and are used widely by different organizations. Due to network effects, the more organizations that use a common set of terminology to describe content attributes, the more valuable the terminology becomes, since everyone has a common basis for locating and exchanging content using this terminology.

Some services like iTunes that allow content creators to submit their content will provide a list of categories to use to classify the topic of the content. In other cases, the creator of the content is required to supply their own terms, and may want to know they are using a term that is widely used and understood. In such a case they will want to explore if any standard list of terms known as controlled vocabularies exist they can reuse.

By reusing an existing vocabulary, publishers can reduce the effort needed to describe the content. They don't need to decide how to describe something; they only need to decide what term to use. External vocabularies are generally high quality and considered authoritative, due to the range of parties involved in their creation, and the fact that their widespread use helps to validate that terms are appropriate to needs. A standard vocabulary ensures that the content producer doesn't use an obscure or non-standard term that might hinder the clarity of information in the metadata. For example, in many parts of the world, the spelling or naming of geographic names undergoes change. It is important to use precise and current names.

No single source is likely to have a list of all the terms needed to describe your content. But publishers can utilize vocabularies from different sources to address their descriptive needs.

Another benefit of external controlled vocabularies is that most have public metadata schemas, so that the text values are not only consistent, they are machine readable across different IT systems.

Widely-used Controlled Vocabularies

Many publicly available controlled vocabularies exist, and are available for publishers to adopt. Some controlled vocabularies have a de facto standard status.

In some cases, corporations or other organizations create controlled vocabularies for their own use, and permit other organizations to adopt their list as a gesture of goodwill. In other cases, organizations such as governments and industry associations have a strategic interest in promoting a common way of describing entities, and hope that a standardized terminology will increase the sharing and reuse of information.

Geographic Names

Geographic locations can be described precisely by longitude and latitude. But people think of a location as having an identity, and sometimes the terms they use to describe that identity varies. The single place can sometimes be referred to by different names, and a place name sometimes will have variant spellings.

Place name variation is an especially large issue when dealing with international place names. It is important to have an internal name standard, so that alternative names can reliably and accurately be displayed to different audiences.

- **U.S. Board on Geographic Names**

In the United States, places are sometimes referred to by different names for various reasons. For example, people may use a posh sounding name associated with someplace desirable that's nearby, or they use an informal name to describe a community that isn't an official jurisdiction.

In order to be able to cross-reference US place entities mentioned in content with other information about those places, it is recommended to use official place names. The official arbiter of current place names in the US is the US Board on Geographic Names.[139]

- **Getty's Thesaurus of Geographic Names**

The Getty Museum catalogs art works from around the world that were created in many different time periods.[140] Both place names and boundaries change throughout history, so Getty has developed a thesaurus indicating preferred terms for different administrative and physical geographic entities.

Simple Product Listing™ from GS1 US

The Simple Product Listing is a vocabulary to describe consumer products using standardized terms.[141] It provides a unique identifier for each product type, a preferred name, and indicates that product variants are included or excluded in the product type. It is being developed by the US unit of GS1, a global commercial standards organization that coordinates B2B data standards such product bar codes.

Medical Subject Headings (MeSH)

MeSH (for **Me**dical **S**ubject **H**eadings) is a controlled vocabulary for biomedical and health-related information, maintained by the US National Library of Medicine.[142] It is used by journals to report research.[143] It is very specific and authoritative, containing 27,000 terms. While oriented to professionals, it maps colloquial terminology to the preferred scientific terminology, so that users can see that "vitamin C" is the equivalent to "ascorbic acid."

The following example discussing the common flu in an article shows how MeSH is used as a controlled vocabulary in the context of schema.org.[144] The entry refers to a controlled vocabulary term (*human influenza*, written as `"Influenza, Human"`) and an associated a code value (D007251).

```
{
```

```
    "@context": "http://schema.org",
    "@id": "http://example.com/article",
    "@type": "ScholarlyArticle",
    "about": {
        "@id":"http://id.nlm.nih.gov/mesh/D00725
1",
        "@type": "InfectiousDisease",
        "name": "Influenza, Human",
        "description": "An acute viral infection
in humans involving the respiratory tract.
It is marked by inflammation of the NASAL
MUCOSA; the PHARYNX; and conjunctiva, and
by headache and severe, often generalized,
myalgia.",
        "code": {
           "@type": "MedicalCode",
           "codeValue": "D007251",
           "codingSystem": "MeSH"
        },
        "mainEntityOfPage": {
             "@id": "#Discussion",
             }
        }
}
```

Literary Genres/Forms

Agreeing on terminology to describe genres of content can be challenging. The Library of Congress has a controlled vocabulary listing 125 genre types.[145] Comics, for example, include biographical comics, detective and mystery comics, and dystopian comics, among others.

Media Topics from IPTC

The International Press Telecommunications Council (IPTC) maintains a controlled vocabulary of 1100 terms relating to topics mentioned in news articles, covering entertainment, business, politics, lifestyle, sports, and weather, among other topics. The taxonomy is up to five levels deep.[146]

Special Case: DBpedia

A machine-readable version of Wikipedia called **DBpedia** is sometimes used to indicate people, organizations, and concepts that are used as metadata values. In effect, all the entries on Wikipedia act like a very large controlled vocabulary that publishers can use in their metadata.

DBpedia draws on the facts listed in the infoboxes[147] in Wikipedia entries to create structured data about entities. DBpedia contains over 4 million entities, including over 1.5 million people. Because of extensive coverage of entities in Wikipedia, DBpedia terms are obvious candidates to identify entities. But it should be used with care, because it's bottom-up governance introduces unique issues for those leveraging DBpedia.

What's Authoritative Can Also Be Changeable. Wikipedia is widely available and utilized, but the topics addressed are subject to change at any time. Due its decentralized governance, its entities are less reliable than controlled vocabularies that are formally created. The presence of an entity in Wikipedia does not signify a consensus what an entity represents, or that it is appropriate for inclusion. Entities in Wikipedia (and by extension DBpedia) sometimes reflect minute distinctions that are not meaningful to general audiences.

Wikipedia entities can disappear if deemed not notable or considered commercially promotional. Entities can merged with others if they seem to overlap with other concepts. While DBpedia resembles a controlled vocabulary, it doesn't quite have the same degree of terminology control associated with planned controlled vocabularies.

Why Stability in Data Values is Important. Like a broken link, a DBpedia entity based on a Wikipedia entry that's been removed can cause problems. So it is best to cite an additional source using the same term, so as to limit the potential for confusion. A common property that's available in metadata schemas is called `sameAs`, which enables the cross-referencing of identifiers use as data values.

A separate, related project known as **Wikidata** also publishing structured data on the web. It has its own system of identifying entities (using numbers starting with the prefix "Q"), which is sometimes referred to as the "QID".[148]

Wikidata is a comparatively new project, and the full range of its application as metadata identifiers is yet to be seen. Its entity identifiers may be more persistent. Because the identifiers are alphanumeric, they are completely independent of any language.

[139] The U.S. Board on Geographic Names, `http://geonames.usgs.gov/domestic/index.html`

[140] "Getty Thesaurus of Geographic Names® Online" `http://www.getty.edu/research/tools/vocabularies/tgn/`

[141] "The GS1 Simple Product Listing™ Standard", GS1 US, `https://www.gs1us.org/resources/standards/gs1-us-simple-product-listing-standard`

[142] "Medical Subject Headings" US National Library of Medicine. `https://www.nlm.nih.gov/mesh/`

[143] N. Baumann, "How to use the Medical Subject Headings (MeSH)", *International Journal of Clinical Practice*, January 2016, `http://onlinelibrary.wiley.com/doi/10.1111/ijcp.12767/full`

[144] Example from "What is Scholarly HTML?", `http://scholarly.vernacular.io`

[145] List is available at `https://classificationweb.net/approved-subjects/1515.html`

[146] IPTC Media Topics: `https://iptc.org/standards/media-topics/`

[147] A list of Wikipedia infoboxes is available at `https://en.wikipedia.org/wiki/Wikipedia:List_of_infoboxes`

[148] For a brief explanation of Q numbers in Wikidata, see "FAQs" `https://www.wikidata.org/wiki/Help:FAQ`

Differences Between Audience-facing and Enterprise Taxonomies

Many people on a web team will be familiar with the term taxonomy, because their website uses a taxonomy. This familiarity can lead to some confusion and patchy assumptions about the purpose of a taxonomy. Taxonomies can support varied goals, but it is rare that a single taxonomy can support all these goals successfully. Many website taxonomies do a poor job at providing valuable metadata, even when they are good at supporting the user experience. I believe it is most helpful to think about two separate varieties of taxonomies: an *audience*-facing one focused on supporting the user experience, and an *enterprise*-facing one focused on business requirements relating to content published by an enterprise.

As mentioned earlier, external controlled vocabularies offer publishers many benefits. But audience-facing taxonomies rarely utilize external controlled vocabularies. They instead use proprietary ways of organization that can hinder many goals that publishers have. It is important to consider in detail how enterprise and audience taxonomies can differ.

Enterprise Taxonomies

The purpose of enterprise taxonomies is to support metadata management. As taxonomy expert Marjorie Hlava succinctly puts it: "What are taxonomies good for? In a word, metadata".[149] The usefulness of the taxonomy is directly linked to the quality of the metadata that is available.

Taxonomies that support metadata requirements are used to classify entities and attributes described by the metadata. This kind of detail is important for managing specific content interactions in IT platforms such as content prioritization or syndication, and supporting specific business requirements such as analytics, search engine optimization, and social media promotion. These taxonomies may be used for metadata relating to other kinds of enterprise information, and not just for web content.

An enterprise taxonomy is stable, specific, and interoperable. An enterprise taxonomy will provide a canonical or authoritative record about all aspects of the content, whether or not audiences care about these aspects.

Audience-Facing Taxonomies

A different kind taxonomy is typically used to support audience tasks and preferences, rather than to address comprehensive enterprise metadata requirements.

In the past, audience-facing taxonomies were the primary way publishers classified web content. Most publishers only cared about organizing static web pages on a single website, and audience-facing taxonomies were sufficient to do that. Today, taxonomies for web content need to support structured data for search, APIs, detailed business analytics, and multi-channel publishing. Audience-facing terminology is still important, but shouldn't dominate how content is classified overall.[150]

Audiences look for words and phrases that match how they think about what they are trying to do, and how they classify the topics discussed in the content. These taxonomies are sometimes referred to as *display taxonomies*, since they represent the labels and categories that are displayed on the screen.[151] Information architects develop display taxonomies to help users navigate through content. The resulting information architecture provides a model to organize the content according to the user's perspective, helping them find and understand content according to the terms and labels they understand. These labels can at times be idiosyncratic, depending on what appeals to a user segment.[152]

Audience-facing taxonomies can generate navigation such as menu labels, and "topic pages" that dynamically aggregate related information. Audience-facing taxonomies reflect the terminology and interests of the audience, and their level of detail should match how much content that is available at any given time. Audience-facing taxonomies can synthesize content themes – they can simplify the representation of what content is available.

Audience-facing taxonomies can be fluid: terms change depending on what the business wants to emphasize, or how much content is currently being produced on a topic. Task-focused labels such as **How to start** or **Ways to enroll** sometimes vary, according to contexts. How categories may be labeled may differ depending on whether the content appears on the website, in a mobile app, or in a third-party platform. The responsive makeup of audience-facing taxonomies means they are not ideal for providing a persistent and consistent description of content.

Unlike enterprise taxonomies, audience-facing ones are not necessarily stable, specific or interoperable.

How Enterprise and Audience Taxonomies Differ

Audience-facing categories and labels are often called a taxonomy because their labels indicate how parts relate to a whole. What's different (and potentially confusing) about an audience-facing taxonomy compared with enterprise taxonomy is its purpose. An enterprise taxonomy is meant to precisely describe entities and attributes. An audience-facing taxonomy, in contrast, sometimes plays the role of descriptive metadata about things mentioned in the content, but other times can play the role of structural metadata indicating where content belongs within the larger website, such as what section of a website has content relating to themes or audience segments. Audience-facing taxonomies can talk about content at widely different levels of detail, from collections of pages, to complete pages of content, to content segments in pages.

An enterprise's internal terminology tends to be more granular than the navigational terms that audiences encounter. Enterprises care about distinctions that may not be important to audiences and should not be exposed to them. Enterprise taxonomies need to be aligned with industry standards, and with internal business operations. Enterprises need to use descriptions that are easily recognized by other systems, such as search engines.

Audience-facing terminology is often informal, more general, and may have a promotional emphasis to it. For example, users might see products classified under the heading of **new arrivals** or **fresh decorating ideas**, even though these terms are not used in other contexts such as in search engine metadata. The categories and labels that information architects create for audiences can be different than the metadata terms that SEO or business analytics specialists want to track.

Relying on audience-facing taxonomies exclusively can limit what metadata can accomplish. Important details cannot be captured or managed. Only enterprise taxonomies can provide the necessary granularity. For publishers to deliver personalized content recommendations, for example, they must rely on detailed metadata that's far more granular than would typically be associated with thematic labels in the information architecture.

Reconciling Audience and Enterprise Taxonomy Needs

Audience-facing taxonomies are an alternative description of the content, rather than the primary description of it.

Audience perceptions are vitally important considerations when displaying content, but should not dictate how to manage metadata pertaining to the content. Enterprise taxonomies need to be *canonical*, while audience-facing facing taxonomies need to *adapt* to varying contexts. Enterprise taxonomies are part of the *core* metadata layer governing the management of content in the content repository. Audience-facing taxonomies are part of the *surface* layer of the content, which, along with other UI elements, is oriented toward displaying and expressing content, and is changeable.

Fortunately, publishers can use a taxonomy management tool to map the terms audiences encounter to the core enterprise controlled vocabulary. The mapping of terms used by different groups is called a *crosswalk*. Taxonomy management tools can provide a master list of terminology that shows alternative terms used in different systems and contexts.

Where possible, coordinate the audience-facing taxonomy with the controlled vocabulary that's used to describe content internally. Some audience-facing categories will align directly to an enterprise classification. But it is important not to force audience and internal descriptions to be identical when each external customers and internal business owners have different needs. The enterprise taxonomy should list the authoritative term. Various alternative audience-facing terms can be noted as equivalent to the enterprise term, and can used for navigation and labels in published content. Not all audience-facing labels will necessarily involve measurable business outcomes, and may not require metadata management.

---

[149] Marjorie M.K. Hlava, *The Taxobook: Principles and Practices of Taxonomy Construction, Part 2* Morgan & Claypool Publishers, 2015, p. 2

[150] Because many organizations mainly consider the user experience dimension when thinking about taxonomies, they often implement *proprietary taxonomies* that are not compatible with terminology used by other organizations, hindering the interpretation of information contained in the metadata, and the exchange of content between organizations.

[151] On display taxonomies, see Chantal Schweizer,"9 Signs of a Great Display Taxonomy", Earley Information Science, June, 2016, `http://www.earley.com/blog/9-signs-great-display-taxonomy`

[152] Different users will often disagree about what to call terms, as many card sorting exercises reveal. Users may favor different terms depending on their prior knowledge, their profession, their social class, their region, or their age, among other reasons.

Developing a Propriety Enterprise Taxonomy

If an appropriate controlled vocabulary is not available to describe certain attributes of your content, you may choose to develop one of your own. Organizations often develop a controlled vocabulary to describe concepts relating to their content.

There are various forms of classification, so let's review the most commonly used ones. Taxonomies are controlled vocabularies that are hierarchical, consisting of broader and narrower terms. Taxonomies often incorporate a thesaurus that shows related terms (synonyms and variant spellings), which helps to clarify which term is preferred. Ontologies are a related approach that distinguishes concepts according to their properties. For the sake of simplicity, we'll refer to all these kinds of classification systems as taxonomies, since taxonomies provide the foundation of modern classification systems.

When to Develop Own Taxonomy

Generally it is best to develop a proprietary taxonomy only for entities and attributes that are both critical to the purpose of your content, and where naming convention standards and best practices aren't available. Such an approach enables to supplement a standard list of terms with terms unique to their organization. Rather than view vocabularies as a binary "make or buy" decision involving complete self-reliance or complete dependence on others, one can adopt publicly available taxonomies and customize them as required.

A key consideration when developing a proprietary taxonomy is understanding whether metadata descriptions need to be inter-operable with other organizations. An internally developed taxonomy can be appropriate when there is no need to share the classification with other parties. Although internally developed taxonomies can be shared with outside parties, the effort involved with getting multiple parties to follow a proprietary taxonomy can be significant. Exchanging metadata is generally easiest when using widely followed standards, which is why it is best to use common, publicly available taxonomies when possible if multiple parties need to share the same terms and classification.

Assessing Unique Needs

Some entities and attributes will be unique to your content. Perhaps parties outside of your organization do not commonly create content about these entities and attributes. Or perhaps your organization is considered the authoritative source of the terminology, because you have coined the terms being discussed. Let's consider some common types of entities and attributes for which organizations will develop their own controlled vocabularies.

Proprietary Names. Propriety names, such as brand names, trademarks, and service marks, are often used to categorize entities, and should be described within metadata in a consistent and standardized manner, including capitalization and punctuation.

For legal or linguistic reasons, proprietary product names may vary in different national markets – this situation is very common in the pharmaceutical industry, for example. Taxonomies should indicate equivalent names, and required usage of names.

Brand assets can signify meaning in content. Slogans are content elements that can be tracked with metadata. The case-formatting of slogans (sentence case or title case) should be consistent for a language. For example, all slogans in English might be in title case, while all slogans in Italian would be in sentence case.

Product Architecture. All descriptions of products need to be consistent. Products are commonly described by a hierarchical architecture that can indicate:

- The **brand** (*business unit*)
- A **sub-brand** or **make** (*family of products*)
- **Product line** (*portfolio of related products*)
- The **product model** name (*base product*)
- The **product number** or variation.

These distinctions need to be separated appropriately, so that information can be sorted and tracked at the appropriate level of granularity.

Product Categorization (*e.g., Lifestyle Categories*). Businesses sometimes categorize products according to attributes of target buyers. For example, a product or service might be associated with use-attributes such as a lifestyle category or a life-stage. Any strategic, persistent segmentation should be described in a standard manner in metadata.

Proprietary Product Attributes. In some industries, the attributes of products may be proprietary: intended to be not directly comparable with attributes of similar products made by other companies. For example, in the beauty sector, brands often create special colors or scents that are meant to be unique. A company selling makeup may describe shades of eye shadow using a proprietary name. Such attributes should be represented in a controlled vocabulary.

Customer Categorization (*e.g., Membership Level*). Content relating to tiered customer benefits such as membership levels, loyalty perks, and associated service categories (e.g. priority service) need a controlled vocabulary. Customers expect to find content specific to their needs based on how the firm identifies their privileges.

Internal Content Management Applications (*Intranets, DAMs*). Controlled vocabularies can be useful to describe internal lingo of an organization, so that all departments and operating units use a shared vocabulary. For example, the organization may need to tag content internally to designate different tiers of legal disclosure. Contexts where having a common internal vocabulary can be useful include Intranets and Digital Asset Management systems (DAMs).

While such systems are primarily intended for internal users who are familiar with internal lingo, be mindful of potential external factors bearing on the choice of taxonomy terms. Systems may need to incorporate externally sourced content that is already described in a certain way, be accessed by external parties such as business contractors and digital agencies, or follow naming conventions for reasons of legal compliance.

Standardizing Names (Words and Phrases). In addition to the unique terms of an organization, other terms may be used frequently, but inconsistently. Perhaps a concept used within one's organization is referred to more than one way, or is sometimes abbreviated. Such cases should be identified, and the preferred usages should be included in the controlled vocabulary.

Costs and Risks of Proprietary Taxonomies

Developing an internal taxonomy carries costs and risks. It is important to understand and plan for the level of effort required to create a taxonomy, and the commitment required to maintain one.

1. Development Effort

An effective taxonomy requires extensive consultation with stakeholders, which can be time consuming. Consensus is needed so that everyone agrees to use a shared language, and feels it reflects the correct level of detail. The underlying structure of a taxonomy should be relatively stable, so that frequent changes aren't required. IT development resources are needed if the organization wants to publish their controlled vocabulary using a metadata schema to improve machine readability.[153]

2. Maintenance Effort

Once created, taxonomies must be maintained. New terms must be added to reflect new products, services, or initiatives. If the taxonomy becomes dated, and out of alignment with current business needs, it may not be used.

3. Governance Effort

Training may be necessary for those using the controlled vocabulary, especially new hires. The business owner of the taxonomy needs to ensure that a shared commitment continues to using the controlled vocabulary in the face of shifting operational circumstances.[154]

These costs and risks should not discourage organizations from developing taxonomies of their own when they are required. But to the extent organizations can "borrow" existing taxonomies that are developed, maintained and governed by other parties, they will reduce the investment they will need to make, while improving their interoperability with other organizations that use these vocabularies.

When External Vocabularies Are Risky

Relying on an external vocabulary can be risky when one needs to describe a fast-changing topic such as new technologies, but the external vocabulary is slow to update itself to reflect these changes.

While vocabularies defined by industry trade groups are generally quite responsive to making changes, some government-defined vocabularies are slower to update. For example, the government classification of industry sectors, designed for the collection of statistics, is often slow to add new categories relating to information technologies and new services. In such cases, you may need to use alternative descriptions pending the revision of the vocabulary standard.

Harmonizing Internal Terminology

A common enterprise taxonomy allows different parts of an organization to share a common set of terminology to describe entities and properties used in content. It can be an important tool to breaking down internal organizational silos.

Often different parts of an organization use different terminology to refer to entities and properties. The goal is to harmonize these terms into a common vocabulary, and to note any substantive differences in how different divisions in an organization define the scope of what a term refers to.

Various possibilities exist for how different organizational divisions might refer to an entity or property:

- **Exact equivalences**, where different organizational divisions use different terms to refer to the exact same thing

- **Inexact equivalences**, where different divisions use different terms to refer to things that overlap but are not exactly the same

- **Partial equivalences**, where the term used in one division covers a broader scope than the term used in another

- **Single-to-multiple equivalences**, where one division uses a single term, while another division uses multiple terms with finer distinctions

- **Non-equivalence**, where one division uses a term to refer to a concept that is not tracked by another division.[155]

Mapping how different terms-in-use relate to others can help to define preferred terms to use in an enterprise taxonomy, and what distinctions are important to capture.

Taxonomies and the Categorization of Content

Until now, we have been discussing taxonomies for data values associated with metadata attributes. For the most part, we have assumed that the attributes and the entities these values describe are already in place. If we are using an existing metadata schema, the overall manner in which content is categorized is provided for us.

Taxonomies can also play a far-reaching role in how information is categorized and described in general. The right term to use as a value depends on how the attribute expresses a characteristic, and what that attribute is named. The attributes selected for use in the metadata reflect the how entities are categorized, and at what level of detail.

Some web teams make the mistake of creating a taxonomy without considering how it needs to be implemented in metadata. Publisher choices about how to categorize content need to be consistent with the metadata schema used to describe the content. A taxonomy may incorporate a hierarchy of entity types (what properties are associated with different entities), or a hierarchy of properties (distinctions in the level of detail a property addresses), choices that need to be reflected in the metadata schema.[156]

Publishers who develop a comprehensive taxonomy of their own need to consider three things:

1. How to categorize and name **entities**

2. How to characterize these entities with **attributes** (and what to call the attributes)

3. What terms can be used to indicate the **value** of each attribute.

Each of these decisions shapes the taxonomy.[157]

Taxonomies depend on both *categorization* (noting distinctions of interest between groups) and *terminology* (using labels that clearly communicate the distinction).

Taxonomies can be involved to create, and so it is wise to consult a specialized resource that discusses how to create them. Two standards for creating taxonomies contain a wealth of information:

- ANSI/NISO Z39.19-2005: *Guidelines for the Construction, Format, and Management of Monolingual Controlled Vocabularies*

- ISO 25964-1: *Thesauri for Information Retrieval.*

If you are considering developing a taxonomy of your own, you should become familiar with some basic concepts in categorization, such as facets and hierarchies.

Facets

One approach to creating a classification terminology is to explore *facets* (aspects) of a domain: the broad subject discussed in the content. Many web publishers produce content that talks about themselves: their company and its products, or a government department and its services. In such cases, the *domain* that the content addresses is the all the things related to the company or government department discussed in its content. If the publisher is a global newspaper, the domain is far larger, covering all the different kinds of news topics the newspaper publishes content on, from politics to sports to lifestyles. The domain is the scope of the published content that a taxonomy must cover.

Domains can be divided into facets that group together related concepts, which are often the big themes of the domain. Each facet provides a focus for considering the characteristics of a particular dimension of the domain. Since discussion of facets and domains can be conceptual and abstract, we will explore how these concepts can be helpful with an example.

Figure 8.1 shows some facets of a generic business organization. It represents a sort of conceptual sketch that will help us fill out a detailed blueprint for a taxonomy. The business domain is broken into generic facets. Within each facet are different dimensions, where one needs to choose terms to classify various distinctions that are important to represent in metadata. These terms represent conceptual categories that need to be managed or measured. After choosing the categories that are important in the organization's published content, such as entity types that should be represented in metadata, these categories need to be given names. When choosing terms to name the types of entities and entity attributes, organizations need to decide if they should create their own terms, or whether they can use common terms that are used elsewhere.

Figure 8.1

Facets of an Organization Can Help Guide Development of a Taxonomy

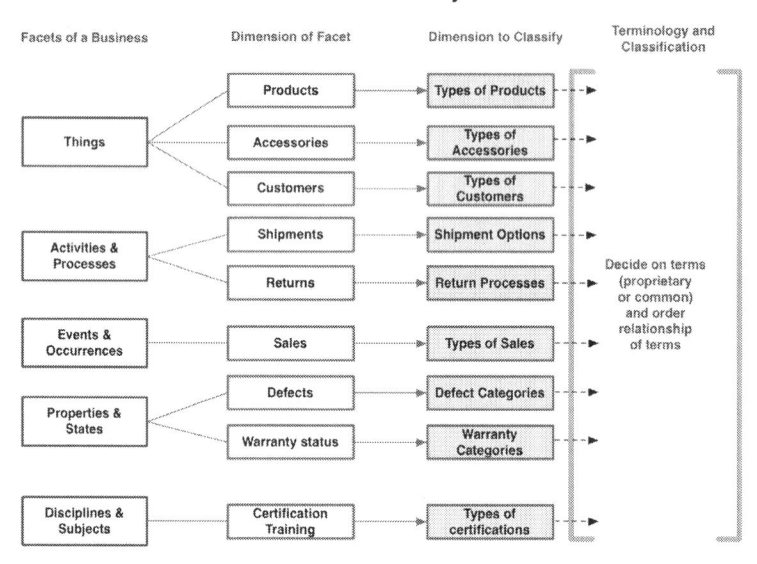

Facets of a Business	Dimension of Facet	Dimension to Classify	Terminology and Classification
Things	Products	Types of Products	
	Accessories	Types of Accessories	
	Customers	Types of Customers	
Activities & Processes	Shipments	Shipment Options	Decide on terms (proprietary or common) and order relationship of terms
	Returns	Return Processes	
Events & Occurrences	Sales	Types of Sales	
Properties & States	Defects	Defect Categories	
	Warranty status	Warranty Categories	
Disciplines & Subjects	Certification Training	Types of certifications	

An important aspect of facets is that each facet is conceptually independent - none of the facets overlap with the others. Each facet provides a description of a part of the whole topic, and all the facets exist in parallel with each other. The terms used in one facet to describe an item can be combined with terms from other facets. When using facets, the full description is achieved through the combination of descriptions from each relevant facet.

Defining Broader and Narrower Relationships

In addition to deciding on appropriate terms to represent concepts to classify, the developer of the taxonomy needs to arrange these concepts hierarchically, into broader and narrower concepts. This task is important because it makes explicit the relationship between different terms. For example, a company may sell breakfast cereal and oatmeal. What is the relationship between these two terms? Are they alternative products, or is oatmeal a sub-category of breakfast cereal? Such choices can have implications for how content is presented, discovered, and tracked.

Increasingly, taxonomies are becoming more precise about the way concepts relate to each other. The more explicitly the taxonomy indicates in what way an item is narrower than its parent, the more able computer programs can tabulate information about entities, by "rolling up" entities into summaries, and breaking down items into more granular levels that represent the same kinds of description.

Taxonomies can represent three varieties of narrower terms:

- **Narrower term (*generic*)**: the narrower term concept is a type of the broader term concept.

- **Narrower term (*partitive*)**: the narrower term concept is a part of the broader term concept.

- **Narrower term (*instance*)**: the narrower term is an instance of the broader term concept.

Figure 8.2

The Relationship between Broader and Narrower Terms

Relating Broader and Narrower Concepts

BTG	Broader term (generic)	← Is A →	Narrower term (generic)	NTG
	Animals	All / Some	Monkeys	

BTP	Broader term (of part)	← Is Part of →	Narrower term (partitive)	NTP
	Eye glasses		Lens	

BTI	Broader term (of instance)	← Is an Instance Of →	Narrower term (instance)	NTI
	Rivers		Hudson	

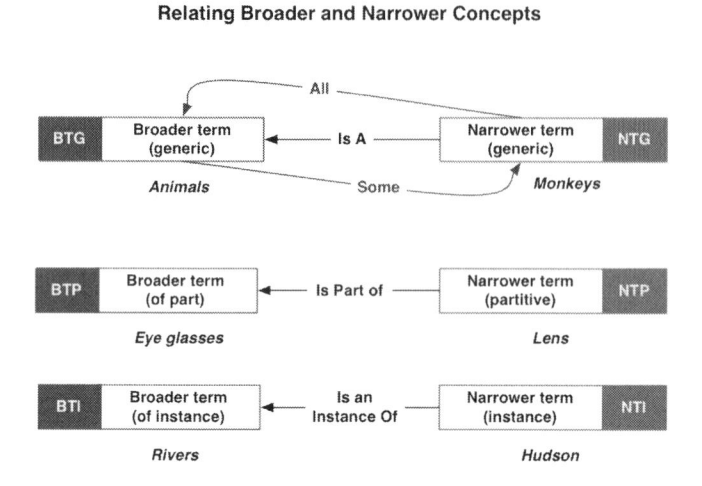

Figure 8.2 illustrates these different kinds of relationships that can exist in a taxonomy. Simply saying a term is broader or narrower than another is often not helpful, since it can obscure important details of the relationship. We need to know if the narrower term of the broader term is of the same entity type, that is, a more specific description for the same general concept, such as monkeys being a type of animal. The number of times monkeys are mentioned in the content will be included in the total number of mentions for all types of animals.

Alternatively, the narrower term might represent a part of the broader term, such as lenses being part of eyeglasses. The number of mentions of lenses in the content has no bearing on the total number of mentions of eyeglasses. But tracking these different but related terms might indicate how important lenses are to the broader topic of eyeglasses. Finally, the narrower term may be an instance of broader term. Instances represent proper nouns or uniquely identified items; they will always be at the bottom of any terminology hierarchy. The Hudson River is an instance of a river.[158] We can count instances: the Hudson is one river mentioned in the content. We can use this relationship to track what specific instances relating to a broader concept might be mentioned in content.

Figure 8.3

The Difference between Instances, Parts, and Generics

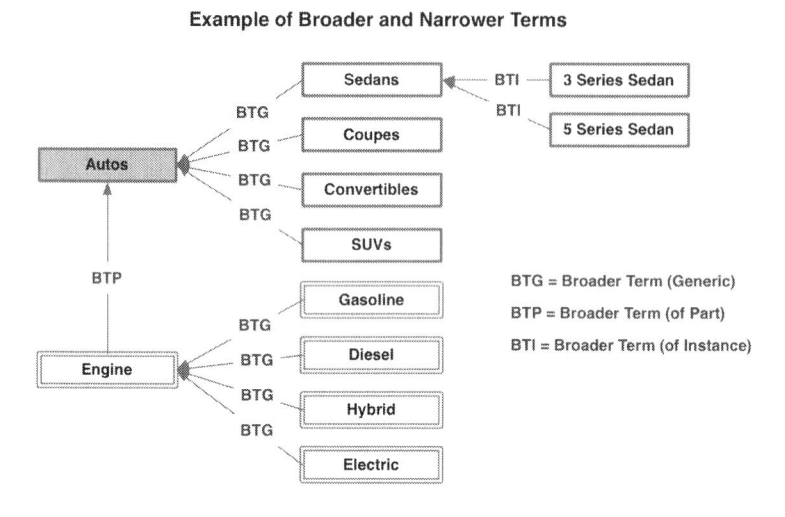

Example of Broader and Narrower Terms

- Autos
  - BTG → Sedans
    - BTI → 3 Series Sedan
    - BTI → 5 Series Sedan
  - BTG → Coupes
  - BTG → Convertibles
  - BTG → SUVs
- Engine (BTP → Autos)
  - BTG → Gasoline
  - BTG → Diesel
  - BTG → Hybrid
  - BTG → Electric

BTG = Broader Term (Generic)
BTP = Broader Term (of Part)
BTI = Broader Term (of Instance)

Let's look at how these distinct broader/narrower relationships can be applied to a specific domain. Figure 8.3 illustrates different kinds of broader and narrower relationships using an example showing levels of description relating to automobiles. On the far right of the diagram are instances of automobiles, the names of specific models. The center column shows category terms: on the top, terms for categories of autos. A convertible is a type of auto. We can see that the models in the diagram are instances of the broader generic term of sedans. In the lower center of the diagram are category terms for types of engines. The term engine is a broader generic term for each of these more narrow categories. Finally, on the left side of the diagram, we can see that an engine is part of autos.

246

As we will see, the automobile example can also illustrate two other aspects of taxonomies: boundaries and naming. The boundaries for groups of concepts affect the naming of the groups, and the naming of the group can influence how the boundaries are perceived.

Boundaries: Developing Categories

A taxonomy reflects how a publisher categorizes its content: the attributes in the content it wants to manage or track, and the detail concerning entities it considers important to specify in metadata. Getting categories right is important, and not always easy.

Distinctions among categories should be comprehensive and mutually exclusive, so that authors understand what category something belongs to. In `Figure 8.3`, we can see categories for types of engines. We would expect all types of engines to be covered, and that there would be no confusion about whether an engine belonged to one type verses another. From the categories listed, we are confident that none of the cars have hydrogen engines, for example. The categories represented are also logically equivalent, each representing an alternate engine technology. Logical equivalence is not always required in taxonomy categories — such as cases where categories represent things not elsewhere specified — but the goal of logical equivalence is a good one to aim for.

A combination of a top-down approach (soliciting views from subject matter experts) and a bottom-up approach (performing an analysis of themes appearing in the content itself) can be used to identify candidate categories.

The taxonomy should accurately reflect the domain it covers. Category coverage should avoid duplication or omission. It should be balanced in its coverage of topics in terms of breadth and depth, to avoid having similar items discussed at different levels of detail. It is helpful to establish a level of significance for including a category, such as frequently topics or ideas are mentioned in the content, or business criticality of the concept.

A perennial issue is knowing how granular to make the taxonomy. Is it okay to just use broader terms, or does the publisher need very specific terms?

Some taxonomies will be broad, where they use big categories, and squeeze different concepts into fewer categories. Broad categories can often be easier for content creators to use, and they can provide a high level summary about content on loosely related topics that might otherwise be difficult to track and manage. Narrow categories can provide more detail. Because of distinctions made by narrower categories, publishers using more granular taxonomies have more knowledge in what specifically is being referenced in the content, and more control over how content can be used and delivered.

Choosing the right level of granularity depends on what the publisher wants to measure and what they want to do with the content.

Naming: Developing Terms

Choosing the right terms for a taxonomy is another important consideration. The names chosen need to match the categories represented in the taxonomy. Returning to the example of automobile engines in Figure 8.3, suppose someone wanted to call an engine that has partial or completely zero emissions as "climate friendly" to focus more on the benefits of the engine instead of its underlying technology. One might wonder how the term climate friendly relates to the concepts of a hybrid engine and electric engine, and if such a term would change the overall categorization.[159] To prevent a misalignment of categorization and terminology, it is best to start by identifying concepts to represent in a taxonomy and then choose names, rather than have the naming of terms precede the development of categories.

Two issues frequently arise when developing terms. First, when should terms be broken into distinct attributes? Second, should terms be in plural or the singular?

Teams working on taxonomies may wonder about the tradeoff between having fewer attributes but requiring more distinct taxonomy terms, or possibly having more attributes but needing fewer taxonomy terms. For example, suppose you needed taxonomy terms to describe sun screen products. You could have one attribute field for product type, and using various terms for different format variations such as "sun screen cream tube", "sun screen spray bottle", "sun screen stick", and so on. Or you might break out distinct elements occurring these phrases into separate attributes, perhaps physical characteristics such as the texture and the type of product container. The right decision will depend on the range of variation in the types, and how regular that variation is. When the terms used to describe attributes follow predictable variations composed from combinations of specific words, it may indicate that will be useful to break these words into discrete taxonomy terms that will be used separate attributes.

Another common decision in taxonomies is whether to use the single or plural form a term. Generally, the plural name will be a better fit for names that are "count nouns" where one can ask how many of an item exists, while the single form is used for mass nouns, where one asks how much of an item exists.[160]

---

[153] Controlled vocabularies can be expressed in a metadata schema called SKOS, the Simple Knowledge Organization System. SKOS descriptions of terms can work in conjunction with public metadata schemas that define entity types and their properties. How to implement SKOS is outside the scope of this book but interested readers can consult the SKOS documentation: "SKOS Simple Knowledge Organization System Reference", W3C Recommendation, August 2009, http://www.w3.org/TR/2009/REC-skos-reference-20090818/

[154] For a good discussion of taxonomy governance, and how it differs from taxonomy maintenance, see Heather Hedden, *The Accidental Taxonomist*, Information Today, 2010, chapter 10.

[155] "Degrees of Equivalence" terminology adapted from thesauri discussion in Jean Aitchison, Alan Gilchrist and David Bawden's book *Thesaurus Construction and Use*, p. 141

[156] How to create or extend a metadata schema is a highly technical topic and outside the scope of this book. The important point to remember is that comprehensive taxonomies should not be developed in isolation from the metadata schema in which they will be implemented. Generally it is ideal to work with an existing metadata schema as a framework for deciding the entities and attributes to address in a taxonomy.

[157] Some simpler taxonomies don't make explicit distinctions between terms that refer to the names of entities, terms that refer to the names of attributes, and terms that refer to permitted values for attributes. But comprehensive taxonomies should explicitly indicate these details.

[158] Note that the diagram reflects a convention in metadata that commonly expresses the relationship description in the singular, even though the entities are often written in the plural. When discussing relationships in sentences, I will use grammatically correct syntax.

[159] A difference choice would be to make "climate friendly" a term for an attribute of engine, rather than a term for a type of engine.

[160] For more detailed guidance, see ANSI/NISO Z39.19-2005 (R2010), *Guidelines for the Construction, Format, and Management of Monolingual Controlled Vocabularies*, section 6.5, http://www.niso.org/apps/group_public/download.php/12591/z39-19-2005r2010.pdf

Chapter 9. Formatting & Standardizing Data Values

Chapter Preview

Metadata concerns capturing details that are important in web content. So it is essential to get those details precise. Data values associated with metadata attributes need to be formatted consistently. In this chapter, formatting refers to how the characters that represent the attribute value are expressed, such as their ordering, and their use of punctuation, symbols, abbreviations and capitalization.
All kinds of values require consistent and precise formats: text values, as well as different kinds of numeric values such as quantities, dates, prices, and geographic coordinates. IT systems depend on precise and predictable values to transform content and make content more dynamic, by automating assessments of the content to reveal content popularity and provide recommendations, and by enabling online audiences to explore content interactively and complete tasks using information in the metadata.
A wide variety of public standards are available that provide guidance on how to specify values. Some values, such as dates and times, follow strict standards that are nearly universally adopted. Other public standards offer guidelines that are considered good practices to follow. A range of public standards exists that provide ID-like values to use in conjunction with text values. ID values such international product codes, clarify what an attribute such

as a product name refers to — especially helpful when a product's name changes in different regions or in different languages.

Other standardized codes are important to indicate regional variations in content, such as indicating target country, language used, and currencies specified.

A Question of Character

To a computer, a character isn't trivial. The range of characters that computers can process keeps expanding. Unicode has thousands of letters, ideograms, syllabograms, punctuation marks, diacritics, and symbols, including a growing range of emoji. These characters can be joined together in countless combinations, creating plenty of opportunity for ambiguity. That's why formatting and standardizing values is important.

Controlled vocabularies indicate what text values to use with attributes, but they don't necessarily indicate how to format these values. For example, the controlled vocabulary might include the phrase **mergers and acquisitions**. Without guidelines for formatting values, some people might write **Mergers & Acquisitions** using capital letters and an ampersand, since that's what's used in the abbreviation M&A.

Even when an organization has a standard on what value to use to describe an attribute, it still needs to ensure that value is formatted correctly. Text and number values that seem the same to humans can sometimes appear different to computers, due to sometimes subtle variations in formatting. Data value formats in metadata are similar to copy editing in writing: both are concerned with ensuring consistency and clarity.

This chapter covers approaches to the formatting and standardization of text values, as well as various types of numeric values and ID-type values. Fortunately computers can help authors with dealing with many of these low-level details, provided the handling of these details was planned for.[161] In some other cases, authors adding metadata descriptions need to be aware of problematic areas, and consistently follow practices that would be indicated in a style guide.[162]

---

[161] The simplest technique is to make sure items in pick-lists of values are formatted in a consistent manner. For many controlled vocabulary values, pick lists are used when authors need to manually select an appropriate value for an attribute. For more open-ended values, IT systems can validate that the value conforms to an expected pattern, as will be discussed later in this chapter.

[162] Many kinds of style guides exist, some with an editorial focus, some with a web development focus. Where metadata guidelines belong will partly depend on your organization's workflow and how responsibilities are distributed. For

organizations that have heavy metadata requirements, it is possible to develop a style guide specifically oriented to metadata requirements. For a example of such a style guide, see Music Business Association, "Music Metadata Style Guide", `https://musicbiz.org/wp-content/uploads/2016/04/MusicMetadataStyleGuide-MusicBiz-FINAL2.0.pdf` While style guides are typically compiled into a document of some kind, the guidelines themselves can be available as short on-screen instructions appearing beside a metadata field to fill-in.

Why the Format of Data Values Matter

Computers can be extremely literal. When strings of characters don't match exactly, computer programs can assume these strings refer to different things, even when they display similarly on the screen. For example, there can be multiple ways to enter an accented character — adding an accent to a letter, or choosing a letter with the accent embedded within it. In some computer programs, those characters, while appearing identical on the screen, are treated as different items.

Consistency

Consistently formatted values are important for many common computer tasks. Computer programs need to be able to identify what values are the same, so they can group items with similar values together, and provide an accurate alphabetical, chronological or numeric sorting of items based on the values entered for the attributes. Consistency enables computer programs to know with certainty that two values are in fact equivalent.

When values are formatted inconsistently, computers often assume the values are different. A music trade association has highlighted some common ways that different people enter the names of music artists. Some will put within parenthesis beside a name of an individual the name of their band, or their birth and death dates, or their instrument. Some will enter the name as last name then first name instead of first name then last name. Spelling errors are also common.[163] All these variations make the metadata difficult to use.

Example: Ordering of Multi-Word Names

Many values will be two or more words. These might be written using different syntax (word arrangement). Suppose the value concerns cheese not made from milk. Is the value represented as **non-dairy cheese** or as **cheese — non-dairy**? In the first case, the value will be next to other non-dairy items in an alphabetical list, such as non-dairy cream and non-dairy yogurt. In the second case, the item will be next to other kinds of cheese, such as **cheese — goat's milk**, or **cheese — sheep's milk**. This decision is known as the pre- and post-coordination of terms.[164]

One of the most vexing coordination issues involves personal names. Often, an attribute for a personal name, such as who the author is, will accommodate a complete name, rather than break out surname, given names, and suffixes. When considered on a global level, personal names involve considerable variation, in terms of composition and ordering. The W3C has a good discussion of the issues involved that need to be considered.[165]

Intelligibility to machines

The ability of computers to perform useful calculations with the information described by the metadata will depend on that description conforming to a format type that the computer understands.

Data Types & Data Formats

Any value with a numeric dimension, such as price, or a date, or a quantity, needs to indicate to computer programs sort of value that it is, which is referred to a *data type*. Data types are more specific than data formats. Data types tell the computer what kinds of operations can be performed on the value. Data formats relate to how data is inputted and displayed. Data types and data formats work together to make data values precise.

For example, a date is a specific data type. Date values are encoded differently than other numbers so software programs recognize the kinds of operations allowed. If the date is the first day of February, and one wants to add 29 days to date, the computer system will know that the new date will be the first or second of March, depending on whether it is a leap year. Dates can be formatted different ways when presented to audiences (for example, with slashes, dots, or hyphens, and in different orderings of the day, month and year.) However, metadata standards for dates are strict about how date values must be formatted when encoded, as will be discussed shortly. In the case of dates, not only must the date be identified as a date data type, the value inputted needs to be in a specific format to be valid.

Other data types, especially text data types, may permit values having a range of formatting (e.g., the use of punctuation and special characters). In these cases, the consistency in the formatting of inputted data values will determine whether software can process the information accurately. The responsibility of ensuring high quality metadata rests with the creator of the metadata, who must make sure they are inputting the values in a consistent format.

Number Formats

Differences in how numeric values are formatted can be significant when dealing with metadata addressing content that is globally sourced and managed.

Different conventions are used for format numbers. Countries follow differing practices for separating decimals and thousands. Some applications add padding to numbers, such as leading or trailing zeros, to make the length of figures consistent.[166]

The following numbers may all be equivalent, depending on the formatting conventions they have followed:

```
1,234,567.89
01234567.89
1 234 567.89
1.234.567,89
1 234 567,890
```

In India, numbers over one hundred thousand are formatted by separating every two digits, in the pattern ##,##,##,##,###, instead of every three digits as is conventional in the most of rest of the world. Thus the number one million is formatted as 10,00,000 in India and 10 million is formatted as 1,00,00,000.[167]

Converting numbers between formats is generally simple, providing all numbers are formatted consistently. If numeric information is obtained from different sources that use different conventions, the needs for data clean up are greater.

Sharing Values Across Applications

When values are formatted consistently, and in a manner that computers understand (i.e., the data is typed), the values can be processed and shared with other applications. When the value used for the location for an event is written in a non-standard format, other computer programs will have difficulty using that information. But when a location value is written in a standard format, different computer applications can share the information. This standardization of values allows one to view a description of the location on a website, and view the location on a map in a separate application, because both the website and the application understand the value in the same way.

---

[163] *ibid.*

[164] This topic can generate spirited debates among people who work with taxonomies. Both approaches have advantages and disadvantages. Coordination influences the sorting of terms, such as where they appear on a menu list. If the terms appear in a hierarchical taxonomy, the parent term will be identifiable regardless of which approach is used. Often, if the entire phrase is familiar to most people, then pre-coordination will be more natural, but if people rarely think about distinctions within categories, then post-coordination can be easier for some people to use. It is important to choose only one approach for all terms, however.

[165] "Personal names around the world" W3C Internationalization, August 2011, `http://www.w3.org/International/questions/qa-personal-names`

[166] For a discussion of number formatting, see "Unicode Locale Data Markup Language (Ldml) Part 3: Numbers", `http://www.unicode.org/reports/tr35/tr35-numbers.html#Formatting`

[167] "Indian numbering system", Wikipedia, `https://en.wikipedia.org/wiki/Indian_numbering_system`

Enforcing Value Formats

Consistent formatting is accomplished through clear guidelines for content creators, and by designing content management systems to provide valid values, and to check that values entered are consistent with formatting rules.

Guidelines for Metadata Creators

People entering metadata need clear guidelines how to enter it in the proper format. This is especially true when the value may be embedded in the body of the content, and the metadata is simply annotating the body of the text.

1. **Character Formatting and Delineators**

Text values many contain characters that imply semantic meaning, such as periods, commas, colons, or semicolons. Such punctuation marks are known as *delineators*. Computer code sometimes looks for delineators as clues.

Programs may have instructions to take content before or after a certain punctuation mark. For example, a book title may contain a subtitle, which appears after a colon. In contexts that don't allow the display of long titles, the computer program may decide to display only the part of the title that appears before the colon.

2. **Names of People and Organizations**

Personal names should be formatted consistently, especially when initials are included in the name.

3. **Composite Values**

Composite values are widespread. They may refer to values that are expressed as pairs, or quantities that indicate the rate of an activity. Examples include:

- describing the resolution of a computer screen as 1920 **by** 1080 pixel resolution

- listing the fuel efficiency of a vehicle as 42 miles **per** (one) gallon

- indicating for a landmark the number of visitors **per year** as 2.3 million

It is important that such values be formatted in a manner that allows them to be compared. While the composite value needs to be displayed in its entirety to be meaningful to users, the value when represented in metadata should be broken into components to enable operations such as ordering and conversion.

Computer Validation

Computer programs can validate certain values to make sure they comply with expected formats. For example, users when entering an email address on a form will have the format of the address checked to ensure it includes the @ sign, followed by character string representing a domain name followed a period, by a recognized top level domain such as com.[168]

The metadata schema used may have expected data types associated with an attribute. If an improper value is entered, the structured data will not validate properly. External validation, checking conformance to the metadata schema, ensures that the data values will be recognized and can be exchanged with other parties. It is especially important for SEO.

However, in many cases the requirements of popular metadata schemas regarding the formatting of values is lax. Many entities allow *any* value to be entered as string literals, and no validation occurs. In such cases the metadata schema validation is not sufficient to assure the quality of the data, and additional internal validation is recommended. Internal validation within a publisher's own IT systems (especially during metadata entry) improves metadata quality, making content easier to manage, and analytics data more useful.

1. **Defining a Data Type**

Different content management systems and metadata schemas vary in the data types they support. Some data types are more specific than others. Common ones associated with web content are a string of text, email address, a phone number, whole number, decimal number, a date, a web address, a graphic file, a video file, and other media formats.[169] The data type may indicate the format required for values, but not always.

2. **Defining Allowable Values**

Computer applications can enforce certain rules, such as making sure that the first word is always capitalized. In addition to rules designed to promote consistency, it is possible to incorporate business rules into the value, so that only certain values are permitted. This kind of validation is similar to the feedback one gets online when creating a password. The system tells the user as they are entering a value in the field if the field doesn't meet certain criteria.

3. Validating Numbers

Numbers are especially important to validate. Computer applications can enforce rules around what numeric values are entered. It might set a minimum value, so that the price is never zero. An attribute might similarly have a maximum value, so that no motorcycle can have more than three wheels. Some numeric values need to be represented as a range, and programs can set parameters concerning the range allowed.

4. Defining Units of Measurement

A special case of number concerns the units of measure. It is useful for computer systems to know the units of measure, so that value can be converted from one measure into another. Common cases include values for food recipes (metric verses imperial, and dry verses liquid), and values for prices in various currencies.

Equating the Audience Description with Computer Values

In many cases how a value is presented to audiences will be the same as how it is described to computers. But in other cases, how these values need to be described will differ. Humans will want something that's easy to read and quick to understand, while computers need very precise descriptions that are hard for people to scan. There are two approaches to bridging this divide.

Equivalent Values

Metadata values can provide clarification when humans think about the values less precisely than computers.

The most common example of equivalent values is when content provides both a human readable value and a second value in the metadata, not visible to humans, that's precise for computers. In HTML data formats, for example, the text of the content presents the value to audiences, but markup around the text can show the content in a machine-understandable format. For example, a precise date can be included within the metadata, while audiences will the date expressed more conversationally.

```
<p>I look forward to next <time
datetime="2018-01-01">New Year's
day</time>.</p>
```

In the case of JSON-LD, the machine-formatted values are in a file that is separate from the audience-facing content.

Equivalent values can ensure that how the value is presented is optimal for both humans and machines. However, care must be taken to ensure that the two values agree with each other, to avoid hidden metadata quality problems.

A popular approach to dealing with variations in how text values are written is to reference a unique ID such as a universal product code, or an authoritative URL. For example, schema.org has a concept it calls *external enumerations* that uses another website URL to indicate a value.[170] To indicate that someone described in the metadata was from the United States, one might declare this with a link to URL of the wikipedia page for the United States:

```
<link itemprop="nationality"
href="http://en.wikipedia.org/wiki/United_Stat
es"/>
```

Referencing URLs is useful in two situations. The first is when a schema defines a limited range of values allowed for a property.[171] The schema provides a precise indication of the value via a URL, even when the text value displayed to audiences may vary in wording.

The second is when an value can reference an authoritative URL such as Wikipedia.[172] This is known as a *canonical URL*. An canonical URL can clarify (or disambiguate) what the value refers to, especially when the URL offers a definition of a term, or provides an "about us" explanation.[173]

Translated Values

For system-generated content, it is common to translate values in machine format into a format audience can easily read. For example, programming libraries such as Moment.js can translate a system-formatted date into a conversational phrase such as **one day ago**. If today's date were April 23, 2017, and the metadata indicated that an article was published on `<time datetime="2017-04-22" />`, the program could interpret the machine readable date and translate it into a verbal statement indicating the article was published one day ago.[174]

Another example is translating geolocation data into a **named place**. The location value is converted to match the current physical context of the online session. Such values have the ability to change dynamically when presented to audiences in different circumstances. An airline might present content that dynamically changes at each airport visited during a passenger's journey to mention the airport's name and information specific to that airport.

---

[168] This kind of validation is commonly done using regular expressions (regex), a programming utility that can find patterns in strings of characters.

[169] Some metadata schemas support an ordered list type, which mandates the sequence order of text values. For example if the

values were called something like "Part I" or "Part II", the data type would make sure that "Part I" always preceded "Part II", assuming the schema specified an ascending order. Ordered lists can be in descending order as well.

[170] "Schema.org markup for external lists", MAY 11, 2012, http://blog.schema.org/2012/05/schemaorg-markup-for-external-lists.html

[171] See the discussion of enumerations in "Getting started with schema.org using Microdata", https://schema.org/docs/gs.html

[172] For a discussion of how external URLs might be used as metadata values, see "WebSchemas/ExternalEnumerations", https://www.w3.org/wiki/WebSchemas/ExternalEnumerations

[173] There may be better alternatives for values if comprehensive machine readability is the primary motivation, however. While search engines such as Google can readily interpret varied URL values, not all IT systems are so oriented. ID-type values will generally be easier for computers to parse.

[174] Documentation on Moment.js is available at http://momentjs.com/docs/

Functionality and Data Formats

Applying standards to value descriptions enables computers to perform operations on these values. Some values describe items verbally with words, others values are numeric, and some values contain a sequence of numbers or letters to identify things uniquely. The ability to compare quantitative values accurately depends on having standardized descriptions that do not overlap so that the same description never refers to two different things. Qualitative values are often paired with alphanumeric identifiers, such as when a book title is linked to an ISBN number for the book. One can count how many books are published with the title *Winning in Business*. But to find out how many of those books are unique, one needs to look at then number of distinct ISBNs of books with that title.

When metadata information from different items is consolidated, the functional potential of metadata can be realized. Provided that metadata descriptions are represented in a consistent manner, the information contained in the metadata can be manipulated in many ways to explain what is in a body of content, and to prioritize how content is delivered.

The diagram below provides an overview of the kinds of operations that can be performed on various kinds of metadata. Metadata involving descriptions and identifiers can be compared and counted. Metadata involving quantitative values can be assessed numerically to rank, filter, and aggregate according to different criteria.

Figure 9.1 provides examples the kinds of metadata associated with different roles.

Figure 9.1

Procedural Possibilities for Different Data Formats

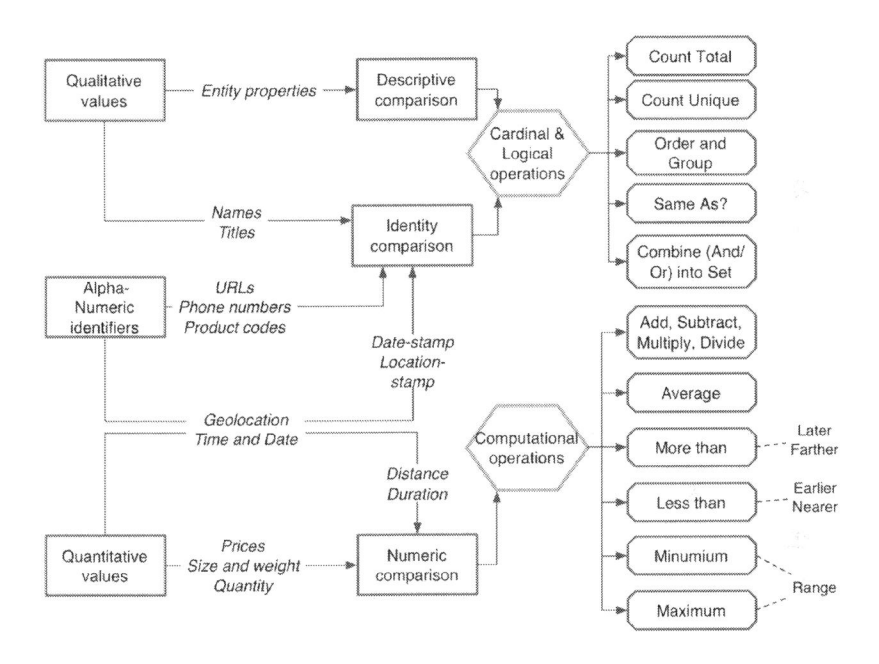

Geolocation values and times and dates are multi-functional. These are quantitative values on which calculations can be performed. But they can also be used to identify entities, because they are more specific than other types of quantitative values. Photos, for example, are often identified with time-stamps and location-stamps.

Location and time data can be converted into distance (from here) or duration (from now until or since) to allow computational operations. The use of time data and location in relation to the user's context allows metadata to support *contextual* content. Common examples include showing content relating to the *nearest* entity, or the *next* available entity.

IT systems use consistently-formatted metadata to *match*, *compare*, *rank* and perform other operations. Publishers can use metadata to support automation in how content is presented to audiences, and to enhance how audiences can interact with the content. While the details of how to implement such functionality goes beyond the scope of this book, it is useful to be aware of some of the potential uses of metadata in enriching the content experience.

Automation

Metadata plays a active role automating what specific content is delivered, and how content elements are displayed. IT systems routinely use metadata to prioritize what content to show to people in news feeds and recommendations.

Automation applies business rules to metadata variables to prioritize content delivery and display. For example, websites can use metadata to deliver customized content based on variables such as the customer's location or the time of year. A website might use geolocation metadata to deliver specialized content relating to the city or even the neighborhood in which the visitor is located. Location data can be associated with content, to enable content to be *location-aware*, so that only content relating specifically to the user's location is presented. Automation can also change the display of content such as greetings and imagery during predefined times of year corresponding to holidays.

Two common approaches to automation are *clustering* and *recommendation systems*. Clustering identifies non-obvious themes in content by assessing content activity in relation to specific metadata variables. A simple example of clustering is when a website highlights **trending topics** by examining on the frequency of new items being created and viewed according to topic.

Recommendation systems can assess the similarity of content according to their metadata characteristics.

Pandora, the streaming music service, provides a recommendation system that uses metadata relating to the characteristics of songs, known as the "Music Genome Project". According to Pandora, this metadata can support a better experience for customers, by matching the characteristics of the music with individual preferences.[175]

Support of User Experience Functionality

The capabilities of computers to aggregate and act on metadata values has a wide-ranging influence on the user's experience when consuming web content.

A recent trend in user experience has been to deemphasize the display of metadata to users. People generally don't see the file size of their documents, or when they were last updated, unless they choose to. Software organizes the content for users, so they don't need to think about the details.

Another trend is toward richer, *on-demand* metadata, such as found in **interactive program guides** for video. With so much content available today to choose from, people expect to be able to locate the kind of content they are interested in quickly.

Metadata can support making content interactive. Content apps and widgets offer audiences the ability to customize the content they are interested in. Auto manufactures, for example, often provide a **configurator widget** that lets people choose the variation of car they desire based on available options.

Metadata can support interactive behaviors that include:

- **Zooming in and out** of a view showing collection of items to show more detail or broader themes.[176]

- **Filtering** a list or set based on some criterion

- Providing **details on demand**, such as tool tips and balloons displaying structured data

- **Extracting variables**, such as being able to download and repurpose calendar date entries.

274

- **Comparing and contrasting** content descriptions according to user defined criteria, such as comparing several images of clothing according color and pattern.

A big benefit of metadata for audiences is that it can help them do tasks across different websites and applications. Information within metadata can often be pushed to another app, or pulled into it. Metadata relating to web content can be integrated with personal data managed in smartphone apps. Customers can perform actions on metadata they view online. They may see an event listing for a fitness meet-up, and book a ticket to the event, and have this data available in their personal calendars and fitness tracking apps.

---

[175] "About The Music Genome Project®", https://www.pandora.com/about/mgp

[176] For example, the kind of behavior that Microsoft refers to as "semantic zoom". See "Semantic zoom", Microsoft Developers Center, https://msdn.microsoft.com/en-us/windows/uwp/controls-and-patterns/semantic-zoom

Key Public Standards for Data Values

Consistency is especially important for specific types of data values that are used widely and repeatedly. Public standards and guidelines for formatting the values have evolved over time to address specific needs, and involve different standards bodies. Some standards address specific domains such as metadata for music, while other standards address generic data types such as dates and times.

Some standards relate to audience-facing presentation of values, but others are codes and identification numbers that are specifically designed for machine-readability, to supplement and clarify descriptions presented to audiences. Some metadata schemas mandate data formats, especially for dates, but in many cases it is up to the content creator to adopt good practices to ensure data consistency.

Despite the diversity of options available to standardize values, we can observe some common approaches used in these options. Options may involve:

- **Guidelines** for how to express text values, such as transliteration standards, or how to format ID-like numeric character sequences, such as phone numbers

- **Standards** establishing machine readable data formats, such as for dates and locations

- **Unique IDs** to help disambiguate text values, such as ISBN numbers representing the title of a book

- **Codes** that differentiate regional variations of content, such as nations, languages and currencies

Languages

Content items should explicitly indicate the language of the content. This is typically administrative metadata that might not be visible to audiences, but will interact with browser settings, and defaults in user applications.

- **ISO 639**

ISO 639 is a family of standards for indicating content language using a two or three character code.[177] In HTML, one can list both a language and a country variation, for example `en-GB` indicates the content is in English as used in Great Britain. For some languages, such as Spanish, one can indicate a regional variation, such as `es-419` to indicate Spanish as used in Latin America.

In some cases a language can be written in more than one script, such as Serbian. One can distinguish Serbian Latin `sr-Latn` from Serbian Cyrillic `sr-Cyrl`. The script code precedes any country-specific identification, so that Montenegrin Serbian written in Cyrillic is encoded as `sr-Cyrl-ME`.

The format of ISO 639 is that the language code is in lower case, any script code will have a capitalized first letter, and any associated country code will be in upper case. For HTML content, these codes are listed in the IANA Language Subtag Registry, with best practices are indicated in BCP 47, Tags for Identifying Languages.

Dates and Times

Standardized dates and times are important because:

1. So many formats are used to display dates and times to humans, both within countries and especially between different countries.

2. Human verbal descriptions of dates and times can be relative to when they were made, and in what time zone they were made.

Two standards for dates and times exist: ISO 8601, and an older standard called RFC 2822.

- **ISO 8601**

ISO 8601 for dates and times is the most widely used metadata standard relating to web content of any kind.[178]

Dates are written in the format YYYY-MM-DD, e.g. 2015-09-25.

Times are expressed in the format HH:MM:SS using a 24-hour clock, e.g. 13:30:00 (the use of minutes and seconds is optional in times). Time zones are optionally indicated as either Z (for Universal Time) or with a +/- HH:MM to indicate shift from Universal Time, e.g., 13:30Z or 13:30-05:00.

Dates and Times can expressed together as a single string, where the start of the time is indicated with a T. Date-time metadata takes the form YYYY-MM-DDTHH:MM:SS, e.g. 2015-09-15T13:30.

- **RFC 2822**

The Internet Message Format has an alternative date and time format. It is mostly used for email and for RSS.[179] The format order is:

```
ddd, DD MMM YYYY HH:mm:ss ZZZZ
```

where:

- o ddd refers to day of the week
- o DD the date
- o MMM the month
- o YYYY the four-digit year
- o HH:mm:ss the time
- o ZZZZ the offset (positive or negative) from Greenwich Mean Time.

For example: `Wed, 02 Oct 2012 08:00:00 -0500`.

Postal Addresses

Postal addresses — and by extension, any physical address — can be challenging to manage, due to the variation in what elements are required, and the order in which they are presented. The issue is significant when presenting content to global audiences, or discussing global locations. Currently, no one standard for describing physical addresses in digital content enjoys worldwide adoption because global variations in address elements make standardization difficult. The best advice is to provide a sufficient level of granularity in addresses to ensure display and exchange of values is accurate.

- **UPU S42**

The Universal Postal Union, a UN agency, created a standard called **S42** that maps all elements used in addresses to the correct syntactical order for different countries.[180] The elements are: Given name, Surname, Street Number, Street Name, Street Type, Floor Number, Town, Region, Postcode, and Country. There are additional sub-elements possible to accommodate specific cases. This mapping of elements can accommodate most common address scenarios in many major countries.[181]

Countries

Countries can sometimes be known by alternative names, or have a long and short name. These variations are removed through the use of country codes.

- ISO 3166

ISO 3166 is a global standard to indicating countries and administrative territories, and exists in three versions. The most common is a two-letter code. For example, Mexico is MX and Singapore is SG.[182]

Geolocation

Geolocation is one of the most important types of metadata, often used in location services. Adding geolocation metadata is referred to as geotagging. It lists the latitude and longitude of a location. The values are translated for audiences to show addresses and indicate locations on maps.

There are alternative formats for geolocation data. As the following example from a Wikipedia article illustrates, many different formats are in use to indicate geolocation values.[183]

```
12.3456, -98.7654
12° 20.736' N, 98° 45.924' W
N 12° 20.736', W 98° 45.924'
12° 20' 44" N, 98° 45' 55" W
N 12° 20' 44", W 98° 45' 55"
```

No one format dominates the encoding geolocation data, though decimal versions are becoming more popular in metadata.

Geotagging is important for many kind of content, being used in different metadata formats and metadata schemas.

For example, geolocation metadata can be included in XMP metadata for photos, and within schema.org as a structured value. In schema.org, geolocation metadata is called *geocoordinates*.[184] The markup would look as follows:

```
<div itemprop="geo" itemscope
itemtype="http://schema.org/GeoCoordinates">
Latitude: 40 deg 44 min 54.36 sec N
Longitude: 73 deg 59 min 8.5 sec W
<meta itemprop="latitude" content="40.75" />
<meta itemprop="longitude" content="-73.98" />
</div>
```

The schema.org example shows how coordinates can be expressed both as minutes of a degree (displayed to audiences), and as decimals values of a degree (structured data invisible to audiences).[185] In the case of decimal expressions of geolocation, locations that are South and West use negative numbers.

Information in one formats can converted into another, as required.

- **GeoNames**

Geonames is an open source database of millions of place names (known formally as "toponyms") that are linked to their geo-location data.[186] Place names include not only cities and towns, but also well-known buildings and natural features such as rivers. Each location has a unique ID, as well as name and geo-coordinates. For example, Rome, the capital of Italy, has an ID of 3169070. Rome can be identified by linking to a Uniform Resource Identifier (URI) of `http://sws.geonames.org/3169070/`. Geonames can display alternate names in different names based on the location and ID.[187]

- **Global Location Number (GS1)**

The Global Location Number from the trade organization GS1 is based on a different structure than coordinate-based systems. Rather than use longitude and latitude, it identifies corporate entities, and then provides "location reference" relating to that specific corporate entity. The 13-digit code can identify both physical locations as well as operational or legal locations. It is designed to describe a precise place or point of contact.[188]

Telephone Numbers

The formatting of telephone numbers can vary according to personal preferences, or local conventions. When presenting telephone numbers to international audiences, it is important that the presentation of the number is unambiguous.

- **E.123**

The International Telecommunications Union, a UN agency, has produced the E.123 standard specifying how to format phone numbers.[189] Two notations exist. A national notation indicates an area code in parenthesis: (607) 123 4567. An international notation which indicates the country code with a + sign: + 22 607 123 4567. The standard does not permit use of punctuation to delimit digits: groups of digits are separated by a space.

Product IDs

Products come in many variations, and description of different products can sound similar. **Global Trade Item Numbers** (GTINs) are a way to give every product a unique identifier, so that people can understand if two descriptions refer to the same or to different products. Such identifiers are becoming mandatory to list products on search engines or on marketplace platforms such as eBay.

Common Product ID Standards/Formats

Product codes are converging into a GTIN common format. With the exception of ISBN and ISSN, all these product codes fall under the oversight of GS1.[190]

- **ISBN**

International Standard Book Number is a 10 or 13 digital identifier for books. The ISBN number indicates the country/language, the publisher, and the title. Serials use a similar but different code called ISSN. A mention of a book title should ideally cross-reference the ISBN, since many book titles are similar.

- **UPC**

Universal Product Code is a 12 digit code used in North America. It is now known as GTIN-12. The code consists of a company prefix (assigned by GS1), a product number, and a "check digit." UPC numbers can be converted to a 13 digit format by adding a zero to be front. Product names and descriptions should cross-reference the UPC to distinguish between similar sounding products.

- **EAN, JAN**

European Article Number (EAN) and Japanese Article Number (JAN) are 13 digit codes originally used in Europe and Japan respectively. They are now known as GTIN-13.

- **GTIN-14**

Global Trade Item Number with 14 digits, where the extra digit indicates packaging.

Personal Names

In select cases, public individuals who create content may have a unique ID that can be associated with their name. These IDs can distinguish between people who share the same surname and given name – a situation that is common in many world languages.

- **International Standard Name Identifier**

The ISNI is a 16-character identifier for people who contribute to media content such as books, TV shows, and newspaper articles.[191]

- **Open Researcher and Contributor ID**

The ORCID is a subset of the ISNI intended for scientific researchers and other academic researchers.[192]

Music

Music metadata is an enormous topic, especially for those who create or publish music. Music identification is important more generally because of two issues. First, nearly all music has intellectual property rights associated with it that needs to be acknowledged appropriately. Second, ambiguity is common when discussing music, since music titles and artists may have similar names, or because different versions exist for piece of music.

- **ISWC**

Musical compositions can be identified with the International Standard Musical Work Code, a standard specified in ISO 15707.

- **ISRC**

Sound recordings of music can be identified with International Standard Recording Code, a standard specified in ISO 3901.

Company names

Company names require special care. Audiences can experience confusion about what entity they are dealing with. Company names can be misleading in many different scenarios.

Some corporations operate in many different markets and in different industries. **Samsung** involves many separate companies from **Samsung Electronics** to **Samsung Heavy Industries** to **Samsung Life Insurance**, each listed separately on the stock market. Some companies are unrelated but have the same name. Ferrari is the name of a maker of sport cars, as well as the name of an unrelated company that makes Italian sparkling wine. Firms also set up separately managed subsidiaries to serve certain markets, so that customers need to locate content from the appropriate subsidiary to be serviced.

Many companies have generic components as part of their names: for example, United, International, Federated, Technologies, Resources, or Services. It is hard for companies to have truly unique names, and as a result, their name can be confused with other organizations. Company identifiers are a way to clarify what company is being referred to.

- **Legal Entity Identifier**

The Legal Entity Identifier is a 20-digit code representing nearly 400,000 public entities. It is a collective, open source initiative, and has been codified in ISO 17442.[193] There are 114 companies with Apple in their name in the LEI. Apple

Inc. (aka Apple Computer) has an LEI ID of HWUPKR0MPOU8FGXBT394.

- **Open PermID** (*Thomson Reuters*)

Thomson Reuters has developed PermID, which provides identifiers for over 3 million organizations globally. It is available under creative commons licensing.[194]

Industry Identifiers

Certain codes are widely used for statistical purposes to collect information relating to activity according to industry sector. These statistical codes are starting to be used in web metadata such as schema.org as well to help identify content relating to specific sectors.

- **The North American Industry Classification System**

NAICS is the dominant industry classification scheme used in North American (USA, Canada, and Mexico).[195] It uses a five or six digit code to describe an industry sector at the most detailed level, though fewer digits can be used to describe broader sectors of industry.

- **UN International Standard Industrial Classification of All Economic Activities**

ISIC is a long-established and universally accepted business classification system administered by the United Nations. It uses a four digit code to identify sectors. The classification helpfully provides details about what specific items are included within a category, and what items are excluded.[196]

Transliteration of Names

Much of the world uses languages that are not written in the Roman alphabet. Generally common nouns are translated, while proper nouns are Romanized. How the names of people and places originally written in non-Latin based languages such as Russian, Korean, Hindi, or Greek can vary, according to specific scheme used to convert these names into the Roman alphabet. This process is called transliteration.

Chinese, Japanese, Russian, and Arabic are some of the more widely used world languages where proper names need to be Romanized when appearing in English.

- **Chinese Transliteration**

Chinese has many dialects. The official dialect of Chinese in China, Taiwan and Singapore is Mandarin, which is transliterated using a system called pinyin, according to ISO 7098, the Romanization of Chinese.[197] The important aspects are capitalization of words, and the separation of polysyllabic phrases, such as "Remin Ribao" (人民日报, the People's Daily newspaper).

- **Japanese Transliteration**

The official standard for Japanese is called the Kunrei Romanization, which is codified as ISO 3602.[198] However, an alternative system called Hepburn is widely used, even by parts of the Japanese government. Either system is acceptable, though mixing systems together is not recommended. Word segmentation is a concern when Romanizing Japanese.[199]

- **Arabic Transliteration**

Arabic has a wide range of transliteration systems, meaning that Arabic names can be written many different ways. There is no universally recognized standard for Romanization of Arabic. The official standard is ISO 233, which is complicated and only used in specialized fields. The ALA-LC system devised by the Library of Congress and the American Library Association offers a more simplified approach that is used by many publishers.

- **Russian Transliteration**

ISO 9 is the official standard. It is precise, and allows for the reconversion of transliterated text back into Cyrillic. The chief limitation of it is that it uses diacritical marks on Latin letters that are not often found in English. An older system called BGN/PCGN is easier for English speakers to recognize and pronounce.

Units of measure

There are hundreds of different units of measure used to describe products and other things.

Some units of measure may be qualified. For example, a measurement could be listed as being a *nominal* value (an actual or precise value), a *maximum* value, or a *minimum* value.

- **UN/CEFACT**

This UN standard covers around 1000 different units of measure using a two or three character code. For example, CEL indicates degrees **Celsius** (°C) while 93 represents **calories per gram** (cal/g). Codes corresponding to less familiar units of measures sometimes have descriptions and/or mathematical definitions that provide a conversion into other measurements.[200]

In schema.org, the unit of measure can be indicated with a property called `unitCode`. Here is an example of how to indicate the unit of measure for **grams**, abbreviated as GRM in CEFACT.[201]

```
<div itemtype="http://schema.org/Product">
<img itemprop="image" src="camera123.jpg" />
<span itemprop="name">Digital Camera 123</span>
<div itemprop="additionalProperty" itemscope itemtype="http://schema.org/PropertyValue">
   <span itemprop="name">Approx. Weight</span>
     <span itemprop="value">450</span>
<meta itemprop="unitCode" content="GRM">g
</div> </div>
```

- **Wikidata**

The Wikidata project has an extensive range of properties covering different types of quantities.[202] A prefix of P followed by a number indicates the type of quantity (e.g.,

P###). For example, to indicate the number of **wins** for a sports team is P1355, while the number of **loses** for a sports team is P1356.

Currencies and Prices

Multiple countries use currencies called dollars, pounds, peso, francs and rupees. ISO 4217 provides codes to indicate the precise currency referenced. For machine-understandability, it is recommended to use a three-letter ISO 4217 code (for example, **USD**) rather than a typographic symbol ($).[203]

Different languages format numbers in different ways. Some languages separate the *cents* associated with a Euro with a coma, while other languages use a period. It is important that all prices be formatted in a common manner. In schema.org, the decimal in prices should be indicated with a full stop (U+002E). Even when the content is written in a language such as Italian that uses a comma to separate euros from cents (e.g., 59,99€), the corresponding metadata should use a period for such numeric values (e.g. 59.99).[204]

[177] A full list is available at "List of ISO 639-1 codes", Wikipedia, https://en.wikipedia.org/wiki/List_of_ISO_639-1_codes

[178] "Date and Time Formats", W3C, http://www.w3.org/TR/NOTE-datetime

[179] "Internet Message Format" https://tools.ietf.org/html/rfc2822

[180] "S42 International Addressing Standards", Universal Postal Union, http://www.upu.int/en/activities/addressing/s42-standard.html

[181] A list of S42 compliant countries is available at http://www.upu.int/en/activities/addressing/s42-standard/compliant-countries.html. Notable countries that are *not* compliant are Russia, India and Japan.

[182] The full list of codes is available on the ISO Online Browsing Platform at https://www.iso.org/obp/ui/#search

[183] "Geotagging", Wikipedia, https://en.wikipedia.org/wiki/Geotagging

[184] "GeoCoordinates", https://schema.org/GeoCoordinates

[185] In addition to formatting the value, another detail is having a shared reference to what the coordinates refer to. Schema.org suggests use of a coordinate standard called WGS (World Geodetic System) 84.

[186] For GeoNames, see http://www.geonames.org

[187] Technical details are available at "GeoNames Ontology", http://www.geonames.org/ontology/documentation.html

[188] Global Location Number, http://www.gs1.org/gln

[189] "E.123 : Notation for national and international telephone numbers, e-mail addresses and web addresses", ITU, https://www.itu.int/rec/T-REC-E.123-200102-I/en

[190] Information covering all the GTIN identifiers available at: http://www.gs1.org/1/gtinrules/en/rule/264/new-product-introduction

[191] "How ISNI Works" ISNI website. http://isni.org/how-isni-works

[192] On ORCID, see http://orcid.org

[193] On the Legal Entity Identifier, see http://www.leiroc.org
[194] Open PermID: https://permid.org
[195] "North American Industry Classification System", http://www.census.gov/eos/www/naics/
[196] "International Standard Industrial Classification of All Economic Activities", Revision 4, 2008, http://unstats.un.org/unsd/publication/seriesM/seriesm_4rev4e.pdf
[197] ISO 7098:2015, "Information and documentation — Romanization of Chinese", http://www.iso.org/iso/catalogue_detail.htm?csnumber=61420
[198] ISO 3602:1989, "Documentation — Romanization of Japanese (kana script)", http://www.iso.org/iso/catalogue_detail.htm?csnumber=9029
[199] The issue of word segmentation in East Asian languages is the topic of another ISO standard, ISO 24614-2:2011, "Language resource management — Word segmentation of written texts — Part 2: Word segmentation for Chinese, Japanese and Korean".
[200] List of CEFACT measures available at http://www.unece.org/fileadmin/DAM/cefact/recommendations/rec20/rec20_rev3_Annex3e.pdf
[201] Example from "WebSchemas/PropertyValuePairs", https://www.w3.org/wiki/WebSchemas/PropertyValuePairs#Point_Value.2C_with_unit_as_UN.2FCEFACT_Common_Code
[202] Wikidata properties: https://www.wikidata.org/wiki/Special:ListProperties/quantity
[203] A list of currency codes is available on Wikipedia, "ISO 4217", https://en.wikipedia.org/wiki/ISO_4217
[204] "prices" https://schema.org/price

Precision and Machine Readability in Descriptions

Between controlled vocabularies and various formatted data values, publishers face many choices on how to describe their content. Let's consider the range of decisions a publisher may need to make, by looking in more detail at an issue that has been cited before as an area of hidden complexity: color.[205]

Many companies offer products in different colors. Some companies even sell products that apply color to other objects: products such as paints and stains. Someone unfamiliar with metadata might be inclined to describe the color of a paint simply with a name, such as crimson red. There is nothing wrong with such a description, but it may not be adequate.

Figure 9.2 presents a diagram showing different dimensions of color. On the far left side are different entities that might need to have their color described. In the center are potential color-related attributes. At the far right are potential values that could represent aspects of color. The question the publisher faces is choosing the right attributes and values based on their web content characteristics.

Figure 9.2

Dimensions of Color: Attribute Value Selection

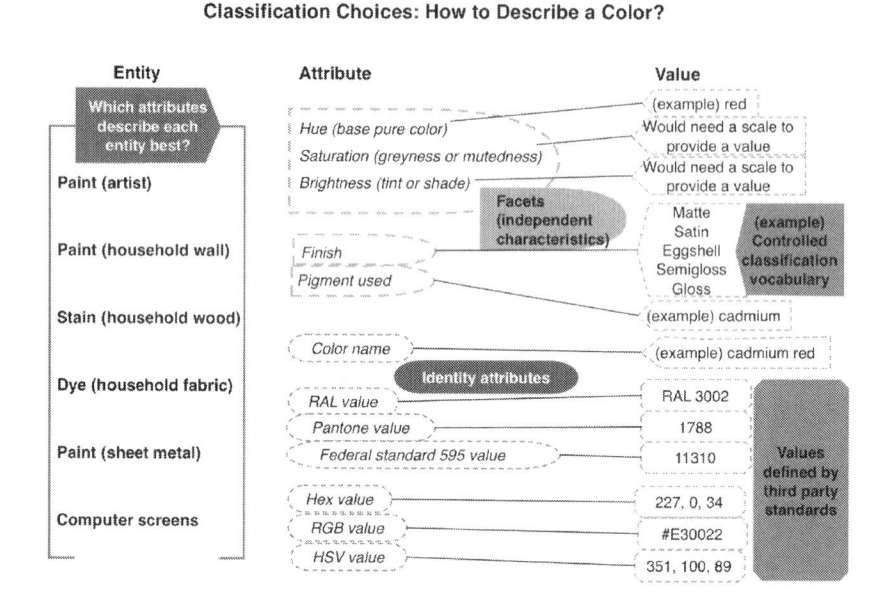

Classification Choices: How to Describe a Color?

Entity	Attribute	Value
Paint (artist)	Hue (base pure color) / Saturation (greyness or mutedness) / Brightness (tint or shade)	(example) red — Would need a scale to provide a value
Paint (household wall)	Finish / Pigment used (Facets — independent characteristics)	Matte, Satin, Eggshell, Semigloss, Gloss (example — Controlled classification vocabulary)
Stain (household wood)	Color name (Identity attributes)	(example) cadmium / (example) cadmium red
Dye (household fabric)	RAL value	RAL 3002
	Pantone value	1788
Paint (sheet metal)	Federal standard 595 value	11310 (Values defined by third party standards)
Computer screens	Hex value	227, 0, 34
	RGB value	#E30022
	HSV value	351, 100, 89

Which attributes describe each entity best?

Several of the entities seem similar. There are various types of paint: wall paint, artist paint, and industrial paint. Stains and dyes sound similar. Can we use any attribute with any of these entities? Actually, paints that have different purposes might be better described using more specific attributes. Some attributes such as color name are generic, but other attributes are closely associated with a specific entity. Artists, when describing color, often refer to facets such as hue, saturation and brightness, each of which could be an attribute related to artist paint.[206] These attributes are not frequently used when describing household wall paint, which is more concerned with the

296

issue of finish, such as whether the paint is glossy. Finish would not generally be a characteristic relevant to other coloring products such as dyes.

The entity that's an outlier on the list is the computer screen. The colors represented on a computer screen are described using very different terms than are used for physical material objects. Colors for a computer screen might be described using a **HEX**, **RGB** or an **HSV** value. So if a color will be presented in digital web content and will be shown on a screen, the correct color must be specified in a format computers will understand. That computer screen description that uses an RGB value needs to correspond to other descriptions of colors relating to paint or other products. We need an accurate equivalence between computer screen color values and other values used. The HSV system (for hue, saturation and value) for computers is conceptually similar to the hue, saturation and brightness facets artists use.

We can describe how a color is made or composed, such as what pigment is used. Descriptions of pigments may be available from an existing controlled vocabulary.

The finish of a household wall paint may involve a controlled vocabulary as well. Each value, such as gloss or semi-gloss, will be distinct, and it will be clear which is appropriate.

Colors generally are given a name, though these names are subject to wide variability. Because of this variability, many manufacturers use different color ID systems to indicate the color more precisely, and will often include corresponding computer screen values in their definitions. **Pantone** is a color ID system that is widely used in the design and home-related fields, but other ID systems are available as well. In Europe a system called **RAL** is used, so that customers in Germany might be expecting to find an RAL value. The US government uses a color ID system called **Federal Standard 595** to specify the color of goods it procures. Each of these ID systems can be a distinct attribute, and each will use a distinct type of value that is governed by an external organization or firm that sets the standards.

The example of color illustrates variations in how concepts are classified and described, especially when the concepts relate to more intangible qualities. Publishers need to consider both the nature of the entities discussed in their content, as well as the needs of their audiences, when choosing attributes to include in their metadata.

---

[205] I am not an expert on color science, which is a intricate discipline that's commercially significant. My purpose is to use color to illustrate issues in metadata, rather than offer advice on how best to specify color characteristics, which will depend on business objectives and metrics, product characteristics, and customer and user requirements.

[206] I am assuming a lazy artist who does not like to mix his own colors and wants paint premixed.

Chapter 10. Cleaning Metadata

CHAPTER PREVIEW

Most organizations have existing web content they have published that already has metadata associated with it. They need to know how useful this metadata is, and what quality problems it may have. Unfortunately, metadata quality problems are common. Metadata can be incomplete, inaccurate, or improperly coded.

Publishers face two tasks: to fix quality problems in their metadata, and to understand how those problems arose so they can prevent them from recurring. Problems can arise from human error and faulty IT setups. Data Values may be inconsistent, exist in duplication, or be erroneous.

Organizations may be unaware of how extensive their metadata quality problems are, and will need to conduct an metadata audit to assess quality. Many instances of quality problems are easily remediated, but sometimes metadata needs to be restructured. Fixing these quality issues requires a team effort, involving both editorial and technical perspectives.

Metadata quality requires an ongoing maintenance effort, to accommodate changing business requirements, and to address changes in external standards and practices.

Working with Existing Metadata

Until now, we have discussed what's involved to create metadata when you don't yet have any, perhaps because there is new project so no content has been published already.

Most organizations already have some metadata relating to their published web content. How good this the existing metadata, and what can be done to make this metadata more useful?

There is a strong chance that at least some of the metadata is unreliable, or incomplete.

The two most common metadata problems are having no metadata describing attributes, and having bad metadata. Bad metadata refers to metadata that is in some way inaccurate. Bad metadata requires cleaning.

Cleaning metadata is similar to fact-checking a story. It involves verifying that values are accurate, and therefore useful. Sometimes values are poorly formatted, as was discussed in `Chapter 9`, but other times the values are formatted properly but they are wrong — they don't describe what they are meant to.

Metadata can be inaccurate for many reasons, and require a range of tasks, both manual and automated, to correct the problems. Fixing metadata problems needs to be a team effort, involving people familiar with both technical and editorial dimensions of content.

Unfortunately there's no single failsafe method to cleaning metadata. But by understanding common problems, publishers can identify the tasks required to fix them.

Why Clean Metadata is Important

Publishers can't know that their existing metadata is *clean* until it has been evaluated for accuracy and completeness. They should never presume their metadata is clean. Bad metadata happens — despite the best of intentions. It is always prudent to assume that some existing metadata is bad, and needs to be fixed.

Defining Good and Bad

The term *bad metadata* is broad and colloquial sounding, but it has the advantage of being able to represent a range of problems that more specific terms might miss. Metadata is bad not due to some subjective opinion of a team member, but because the metadata fails to represent what it needs to, according to agreed requirements.

No single litmus test exists to assess the quality of metadata. However, several dimensions are important:

- **Accuracy** of the description — whether it reflects accurately what's in the content

- **Precision** of the description — the absence of ambiguity, and the right level of detail

- **Completeness of the attributes** used in a description

- **Completeness of the values** included in a description

- Consistency and correctness of the **formatting** of the values

- Timeliness of the **terminology used**, reflecting current content needs

- **Relevance** of the attributes and values **to users** of the metadata

- **Ability of machines** to interpret and process the information

Existing metadata should be evaluated against these criteria. They can form a checklist for metadata quality.

Metadata quality checklist

- ☐ Content item: Description is true

- ☐ Content item: Description is clear (no confusion possible)

- ☐ Content item: Description identifies all important entities

- ☐ Entity: No attributes missing that are needed or useful

- ☐ Entity: No values are missing from attributes

- ☐ Values are formatted correctly

- ☐ Terminology used for attributes and values is current

❏ Attributes and values are relevant to users (internal and external), and aren't superfluous

❏ Values are machine readable to full extent possible

Quality Criteria can be Specific to Organizations. The checklist is generic, and needs to be adapted to the specific requirements of an organization: the goals it has set for its metadata, and the nature of the content it publishes. Business goals for metadata, such as improving content reuse or enabling the sharing of content with business partners, are based on overall content priorities. The specific criteria a publisher sets for metadata quality should focus on the realization of concrete business goals. High priority content should have high quality metadata.

Perfect metadata is hard to achieve, especially if the volume of content published is substantial. The vigilance considered necessary to ensure quality will depend on how critical certain metadata is to an organization. Metadata for some aspects of content needs to be *exhaustive*, while for other areas the metadata only needs to be *serviceable*, and not gold standard quality. For example, search-related metadata can be either very detailed, or only include a few details, depending on the publisher's preferences. If search is important to reach certain audiences, and the content is critical to the business, exhaustive metadata would be advisable. For content that is less business-critical and mostly distributed by email, less detail may be required.

Evaluate Using Common Criteria. It's important that everyone within the organization follow the same standards to assess the quality of existing metadata. Criteria for cleaning existing metadata should be consistent with requirements for new metadata that the entire organization developed and agreed to.

To take one example from the checklist, various publishers will likely have different ideas about what attributes are needed or useful, since they have different priorities and goals. But each specific publisher needs to have their own criteria for such a question that is followed by everyone in their organization, and not leave the choices to individuals who might arrive at different conclusions.

Risk Factors associated with Poor Quality Metadata

When existing metadata is problematic, publishers may feel overwhelmed, and disinclined to fix the problems. By assessing concrete risks associated with poor quality metadata, publishers can prioritize areas of metadata to evaluate. Some of the most business-critical metadata can affect whether customers complete tasks, and whether IT automation can be supported.

Risks to Customer Acquisition and Retention. Faulty metadata may mean customers can't find what they are looking for in your online catalog. Or they might see sloppy or inaccurate descriptions, and wonder about the quality of brand. Missing and inaccurate metadata is a common problem even with the largest online retailers. Sometimes products aren't sold not because customers aren't seeking them, but because they can't find them when are they searching for them.[207]

Risks to Business Expansion Plans. Poor metadata can also stymie strategic initiatives within an organization. It can hold back the rollout of new initiatives, such as implementation of APIs or apps to deliver content more widely. Many organizations discover the importance of solid metadata when they embark on a bold initiative, and discover that the solid foundation required to realize the initiative wasn't in place. The metadata may exist, but its quality wasn't sufficiently reliable to support the automation envisioned.

---

[207] Search logs can sometimes reveal hidden metadata quality problems.

Poor Governance Can Hurt Metadata Quality

Metadata quality problems can indicate a need for better governance of content. Either existing governance practices have created quality problems and suggest the need for better practices, or changing content management requirements are prompting the introduction of new governance measures to manage an emerging quality issue.

Human Error or Neglect. Content producers might enter metadata incorrectly because they lack a controlled vocabulary, or lack sufficient training on how to enter metadata. This problem can be especially common when relying on outside vendors or other parties to provide metadata the publisher will be using.

Merging of Different Systems. Consolidating content from different silos often exposes differences in how various systems used metadata. Different systems may use different attributes, or follow different practices for indicating the values in attributes. For example, an organization may have many different microsites of published content they want to consolidate into a single website. Because each microsite was conceived of and managed separately, each follows different standards for metadata quality and completeness.

Common Problems in Metadata Quality

Unfortunately, the quality of metadata is often off the radar of many organizations. It doesn't get much visibility, and it is rarely seen as an issue involving collective responsibility.

Quality problems are often never anticipated. They might only be revealed when the publisher embarks on a new content initiative, but finds it can't start until it fixes quality problems in its metadata. For example, the process of migrating content from one content management system to another can reveal deficiencies in the metadata. Business owners may want to deliver content in a certain way, but find they don't have metadata to support that goal.

Missing Values

Content producers sometimes consider metadata that is not mandatory as unnecessary. This attitude reflects an under-appreciation of the important functions that metadata supports. Content systems need to be clear which fields are always needed and make those mandatory.

Confusion about When Attributes are Required. Fields don't need to be mandatory. Some fields are conditionally mandatory: a business rule dictates when the field is necessary. Ideally the system can flag that dependency. Other fields are recommended — they support certain tactical goals such as what content gets promotional emphasis, but are not critical to the integrity of the entire corpus of content. Optional fields should be reserved for edge cases, such as when one needs to qualify or supplement information in other fields to increase accuracy. For both recommended and optional fields, the system should indicate when these fields should be used, and what capabilities they support.

Inconsistency in Values

Inconsistent terminology and spelling can reflect governance and implementation issues. It may indicate that a controlled vocabulary is not available, is incomplete or is not being followed. It might indicate that important fields are free text rather than drop down choices. It may also suggest that auto-generation of metadata might be desirable. Finally, spelling mistakes in metadata are common: the entry of metadata information commonly get less oversight than publicly facing content receives, and spelling mistakes may be less conspicuous and escape detection.

Duplication

Duplication of metadata may seem like a minor problem compared with errors. But duplication can hurt analytics measurement and make management of content more difficult. For example, duplicated records make it hard to track the removal of content from public view.

Fields that are Confused. Some metadata fields seem conceptually similar, so that content producers are unclear what the difference between them is. Perhaps the CMS has one field called **topic**, and another called **tags**. When fields seem similar, authors may enter the same value in two different places, or enter information inconsistently. Usability testing of the author interface can help resolve such issues.

Multiple Records for Same Item. Duplicate content is common, and will yield duplicate metadata. It can sometimes be difficult from the metadata to spot what content is duplicate without examining the full content. Duplication hurts the audience experience, and frustrates accurate collection of analytics.

Machine and Human Errors

Errors in metadata can be divided into errors associated with how IT systems code metadata (and how code is interpreted by IT systems), and errors arising from how human enter metadata in content management systems.

Machine Errors

- **Bad Defaults**. Some metadata, especially administrative metadata, is system generated — unless explicitly told otherwise, the system will supply a default value. When the defaults aren't right, the metadata generated is wrong. Common problems include wrong dates, or authors listed as "administrator." If metadata choices are listed in a dropdown menu, it is important that the default option does not generate inaccurate information.

- **Markup Errors.** It is also possible that metadata that was entered appears invisible to computers, due to invalid markup. Some semantic markup in particular can be complex, and needs to be validated thoroughly.

When a third party will need to process metadata created by your organization, it is important that the metadata markup be crosschecked by an outside service. Various services that consume or republish metadata offer tools known as validators or linters to check the technical correctness of the metadata.[208]

- **Machine Classification Errors.** Computer systems can identify entities mentioned in text, and classify metadata automatically. But if this capability is not set up properly, or there is ambiguity as to what the text relates to, the system may generate spurious metadata. In cases where errors are likely to occur, it is best to have humans verify the decisions of the system before it is finalized.

Human Issues: Data Entry and UI Problems

- **Misuse of Fields.** Content producers may misuse metadata fields by putting the wrong kind of information in the field. Such misuse may be the result of confusing labels on in the user interface used to enter metadata, or poor training.

Problems may arise when content producers feel the content management system doesn't offer a feature they need, and they consider an existing field superfluous. They might add personal notes or idiosyncratic codes to a field not related to intended purpose of the field.

- **Field Overloading**. Field overloading occurs when two different values are placed in one field, when they should be in separate fields. Seth van Hooland and Ruben Verborgh note that two kinds of issues can result in field overloading:

    1. When one needs to "encode multiple values of the same type in one field."

    2. When "different realities are described within the same field" because "the content of the field is too generic."[209]

    They cite postal addresses as being classic case of field overloading. The solution to field overloading is to provide enough fields to accommodate distinct entries, and to break fields into subfields when different informational aspects are present.

[208] For a list of validation tools, see the "Resources" listing in the Appendix.

[209] Seth van Hooland and Ruben Verborgh, *Linked Data for Libraries, Archives and Museums*. Neal-Schuman, 2014. pp. 84-85

Approaches to Cleaning Metadata

Cleaning metadata involves assessing the scope of quality issues by auditing the metadata, and once issues have been identified, fixing the problems. Many problems can be fixed by simply adding missing values, or correcting obvious mistakes such as wrong dates, misspelling or inconsistently formatted values. Some problems are more structural, and necessitate a refactoring of the metadata: fundamentally changing the attributes used within the metadata, or the values used for these attributes.

Auditing

Auditing metadata is an important task that is often overlooked. Audits look at metadata used in existing web content and assesses it. The completed assessment provides a listing of metadata that requires remediation.

Metadata audits involve three inputs:

1. The **source content** intended for audiences

2. The **existing metadata** about this content

3. Requirements indicating the **expected quality** for the published metadata.

The existing metadata needs to be compared with the requirements indicating expected quality, and in many cases, with the source content. Suppose product pages typically include prices, but metadata about prices is missing. Generally we would assume that the problem rests with the metadata being incomplete, rather than assume the content is incomplete. But it could be possible that some product pages don't include price information.

Metadata should only reflect what's in the published content. So the published metadata needs to be compared with the published content to assess its completeness. This is especially important when evaluating whether all entities have been included in the metadata that are significant in the content.

When the source content is highly regular in its scope, and familiar to those doing the audit, there is less of a need to refer to it during the metadata audit. Most of the evaluation will focus on the existing metadata, and quality issues will easier to spot.

The Auditing Process. Auditing metadata is similar to auditing content, but with a deeper focus on the attributes and values assigned to the content. The scope of the audit should reflect the business criticality of the metadata, and risks that faulty metadata poses to business outcomes. High priority metadata to audit will be associated with content that is widely viewed by audiences, and content that is associated with important business outcomes, such as pages where customers make decisions.

Once a section of content has been identified for auditing, its metadata can be evaluated against a set of agreed requirements. The quality checklist presented earlier in this chapter provides a basis for a publisher to develop their own list of requirements for the quality of metadata published, such as how important completeness and consistency is for various metadata. The audit will note metadata that does not meet the requirements, and indicate what changes need to be taken, such as correcting or adding values, or adding properties or entities.

Sourcing a Report of Existing Metadata. A report of metadata used can be generated from within some content management systems, or can be generated through a web crawl. Some tools may be able to offer a high level summary of types of metadata used in the content, and identify the extent of missing values.

A separate aspect of an audit concerns markup errors and validation errors. Those issues should be identified by checking existing metadata markup using a validation tool.[210]

Because of the potentially large volume of metadata that may exist, some publishers will need to perform auditing on a rolling basis. The may start looking at the metadata from selection of content addressing a certain topic or produced by a certain division, and then repeat the audit process by looking at metadata from a different selection of content.

Refactoring Metadata

Refactoring is the process of cleaning up code to make it more efficient in delivering what it was intended to deliver. Like other forms of code, metadata can benefit from refactoring. The greater the inconsistency in the metadata, the more work machines need to do to understand the metadata, such as *stemming* to look for words with a common root when different variations of the same basic word are used within the metadata. The goal should be to publish metadata that is straightforward for computers to understand.

Normalization

Normalization means that all items are described in a consistent way. When several different terms have been used that all mean the same thing, the terms need to be normalized using one standard term according to a controlled vocabulary. Some organizations produce a metadata style guide when there may be uncertainty about the preferred way to enter terms.

OpenRefine is a spreadsheet-like tool that is able to do pattern recognition to find items that seem similar. Formerly known as Google Refine, it used to clean all kinds of data, including metadata. It can detect duplicates, transform text to make the formatting consistent, and split descriptions into separate smaller units.

Other tools with similar capabilities are available. Tools with these capabilities are sometimes called *data wrangling* software.

Restructuring Elements

Sometimes elements need to be restructured: for example, if fields are overloaded. Fields need to be able to accommodate as many instances as might be necessary, so that the author field can accommodate more than one author if required. Fields make need to be broken apart, so that location is split into discrete elements of street, city and region. Redundant fields that overlap, or serve no business purpose, should be removed.

Pruning. Organizations need to periodically assess if metadata fields are necessary. They may have been created to serve a specific need that no longer exists. In such cases, the field should be retired from use.

`Figure 10.1` shows how existing metadata categories (entities or attributes) may need to be transformed into new categories through a process known as refactoring.[211]

Figure 10.1

Examples of Refactoring Metadata Categories

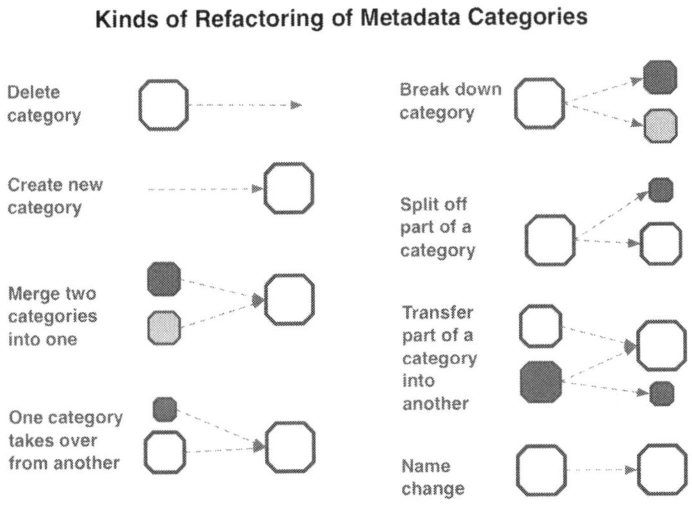

Kinds of Refactoring of Metadata Categories

- Delete category
- Create new category
- Merge two categories into one
- One category takes over from another
- Break down category
- Split off part of a category
- Transfer part of a category into another
- Name change

Ongoing Maintenance

Cleaning and refactoring metadata are vital to improve quality, but metadata requires active maintenance in order for the metadata to stay relevant and be utilized.

All metadata collected should support current and future business goals. Out of date fields and terms should be retired, and new attributes and terms should be added as required. Sometimes the level of detail will need to change: past priorities may have justified extensive metadata detail that no longer makes sense. Often, new needs will require additional detail in metadata descriptions. A concept in metadata called *hospitality* refers to the capacity to grow the terminology used to address changing requirements.[212]

Business owners of metadata should regularly review how metadata requirements may be changing, and plan for ongoing revisions. They should compare existing metadata categories with emerging business requirements, and monitor how changes in the topical and media profiles of content being published may impact the metadata attributes required. Metadata owners should also be mindful of changes in industry and technical standards that will impact metadata collection and implementation practices.

---

[210] A list of tools for different syntaxes is available in the "Resources" listing on the Appendix.

[211] Adapted from the United Nations Economic Commission for Europe (UNECE) "Neuchâtel Terminology Model", available at http://www1.unece.org/stat/platform/pages/viewpage.action?pageId=14319930

[212] On hospitality, see Jean Aitchison, Alan Gilchrist, and David Bawden, *Thesaurus Construction and Use: a Practical Manual*, 4th edition, Europa Publications, 2000, pp. 80-81.

Chapter 11. The Future of Metadata for Web Content

CHAPTER PREVIEW

> Web content is constantly changing. Sensory media such as photos and video is becoming more important to audiences. Publishers want to be able to take advantage of content in any medium, while having precise control over this content. But currently metadata for sensory media is much less granular than it is for text-based content. Some approaches currently under development hint at how publishers could acquire more precise metadata for sensory media content, which would allow them to have more flexibility with such content.

Web Metadata and Digital Media

Metadata practices are constantly evolving to meet new challenges. The biggest challenge for content is the growing volume of unstructured content, especially images, audio and video. Such content is typically a digital file of material where any editorial choices involved with its production aren't captured in metadata. For example, a video or audio published online may be composed of several segments, but what each segment represents isn't represented in metadata.[213]

Visual and audio content are sensory media, which can be more enjoyable for audiences to experience compared with more cognitively demanding content involving text and numbers. Metadata is getting much better with managing text content, but this progress isn't yet evident for sensory media. In many organizations, video in particular is becoming more important, and more robust metadata capabilities are needed.

Some recent industry developments give us a preview of how metadata can play a growing role helping people locate specific aspects for web content that aren't articles and documents. Even if most of your current content is text-based, chances are good that other content formats will play a bigger role for your organization in the future. All kinds of publishers will need better approaches to metadata for media formats that currently lack structure. While this discussion makes no predictions about precisely how or when these challenges will be solved, some of these approaches we will look at could become available as features in IT systems and enterprise software services in the future.

---

[213] Some organizations have detailed metadata about the pieces of media in their digital asset management system that is available internally prior to publication. But it is not common for these details to be published together with the completed video or audio.

Visual Metadata

Images, especially photos, are simple to create, but hard to categorize. The volume of images keeps growing, and finding the right image is getting more challenging.

From the perspective of metadata, the biggest advance has been the development of feature analysis of imagery. People already have the ability to search on features such as color, shape, and texture. Such features can be extracted automatically. The even bigger transformation in metadata for imagery is feature detection. Larger firms such as Facebook are already using face recognition to identify people in photos, and an open source project offering this capability called OpenFace exists.[214] Feature detection can also be used to identify objects in photos, the moods associated with the expression of people in photos, or event related information based on differences in photos of places at different points in time. Every time a computer performs a classification, it needs to be recorded as metadata to provide enduring utility.

---

[214] OpenFace: Face Recognition with Deep Neural Networks
`http://github.com/cmusatyalab/openface`

Granular Video

Video is typically composed of many elements: different clips or segments, and a range of images, soundtracks and captions. Many use cases exist for unbundling an assembled video: to localize content for specific audiences, and to allow retrieval and viewing of specific segments of video pertaining to topic or featuring a certain person. Gaining this flexibility requires more granular metadata.

Video content analysis is a "capability of automatically analyzing video to detect and determine temporal and spatial events."[215] It is one of many developments that open up possibilities for additional metadata enrichment of video content.

The BBC is working on "object based media" that uses metadata to describe how objects can be assembled. "As well as being able to adapt to screen size and device type, object based media would also be able to adapt to the preferences of the viewer."[216]

Another project supporting more granular video is the development of word-timed transcripts. By linking timing metadata for a written transcript and corresponding audio in a video, users can locate a very specific segment of a video.[217]

Granular video metadata will also support advances in web accessibility. Video accessibility is largely focused on supplying subtitles for video. Providing a transcript of video is an important step to enable the exploration and use of video content by those who have a hearing impairment. But text-based transcripts are subject to the same limitations of other written text content, where words can be ambiguous in meaning, and relationships between entities mentioned in the content are not explicit. Eventually, metadata for video content will need to become more entity-focused, relying not just on words to transcribe the audio and to provide a narrative description of visual imagery, but also identifying entities in the video, and revealing how entities are connected to each other and to content elsewhere. The text accompanying a video will need to be enhanced with semantic metadata, something rarely done today. Only then will content in different formats have true parity with respect to their metadata description.

---

[215] "Video Content Analysis", article in Wikipedia.
https://en.wikipedia.org/wiki/Video_content_analysis

[216] Max Leonard, "Forecaster: Our Object-Based Weather Forecast" BBC Research & Development, December 1, 2015.
http://www.bbc.co.uk/rd/blog/2015-11-forecaster-our-experimental-object-based-weather-forecast

[217] Mark Boas, "Spoken Words and Their Timings" BBC Research & Development, May 15, 2015.
http://www.bbc.co.uk/rd/blog/2015-05-spoken-words-and-their-timings

Live Content

Live content represents another challenge for metadata, since it demands extra agility to keep the metadata current. Many organizations are offering content in real time, such as live blogging a conference or event. People and topics mentioned at events may be associated with background content that would be useful to link to. In one commercial example, a firm provides metadata relating to live sports events, continually updating scores, roster changes and schedules. Its services "identify the most interesting plays of the game in real time." It uses metadata to link "live content, notable plays and athlete career highlights."[218]

Metadata for live content benefits from automation in data collection and classification. It also requires planning to anticipate likely scenarios where the need for specific metadata may arise. The best candidates for applying metadata to live content are domains where the entities that will appear in the content are known in advance. Examples include sports, political debates or press conferences on specific topics, financial and technology news, and ceremonial events including parades, political conventions, arts festivals and entertainment awards.

[218] Holly Ashford, "Rovi Launches Sports Metadata to Connect Fans" TVBEurope. January 6, 2016.
http://www.tvbeurope.com/rovi-launches-sports-metadata-to-connect-fans/

Appendix A. Approaches to Turning Metadata into Code

Metadata implementation involves three tasks:

1. **Defining** what metadata is needed
2. **Creating** the metadata information
3. **Implementing** the metadata in code.

This book has focused on knowledge needed to identify what kinds of metadata that are useful, and on how to populate the values for this metadata. The actual coding of metadata is an enormous topic, and often requires programming knowledge beyond the basic HTML skills many people may be familiar with. But for the benefit of readers who interested in how metadata actually gets into computer systems, this appendix offers a *short* overview of approaches.

The approaches used to inject metadata into computer systems are quite varied. They depend on the features and capabilities of content management systems, the choices about data structure and metadata schemas, and architectural decisions such as where the metadata is stored. Different approaches involve distinct workflows.

Five broad approaches to metadata encoding exist:

1. Hand coding

2. Lightweight markup

3. Loading metadata values from an external source

4. Graphical annotation editors

5. Automatic hardcoding.

Hand Coding

Metadata, like other forms of computer code, can be coded using a text editor. The process is similar to coding HTML in a text editor. It is a very direct method, but is not efficient for large content repositories. It is mostly used for small content projects, and as part of software development activities.

Hand coded metadata can be error prone, and needs to be validated, for example, using a data linter.

Lightweight Markup

Metadata code can be hard for humans to read and write. Even HTML is bulky to read and write. In the case of HTML, some light weight markup languages such as Markdown exist that allow people to express HTML attributes using simpler formatting. The markdown is then converted into HTML.

YAML is lightweight markup language similar in concept to Markdown. Unlike Markdown, which is focused on text, YAML is designed to express structured data that might otherwise be coded in JSON. YAML is much simpler to write and read than JSON, relying on indentations to express the relationship between elements. Provided the formatting is correct, the YAML data can be serialized into JSON or XML. YAML is most effective expressing comparatively simple metadata.

Some organizations involved with high volumes of RDF metadata use the Turtle (Terse RDF Triple Language) or N3 syntaxes, which are less verbose than many other syntaxes.

External Loading of Metadata

Certain metadata can be loaded from external files such as spreadsheets. For example, NPR has developed a program called copytext that allows journalists to enter values in a spreadsheet, which are then loaded into a system to be published online.[219] Since spreadsheets are a basic form of structuring data, loading values from spreadsheets can be efficient in certain use cases. Spreadsheets may be especially efficient for the batch loading of values for descriptive metadata.

---

[219] NPR tool:
`http://blog.apps.npr.org/2014/04/21/introducing-copytext-py.html`

Graphical Annotation Editors

Many writers are comfortable with graphical editors that highlight elements in different colors or use visual tags. Metadata annotation capabilities are becoming more common in graphical editors. They are sometimes referred to as WYSIWYM editors, or "what you see is what you mean".[220]

Annotation editors come in many varieties. Some are standalone editors, where the writer will add metadata to a document before it is added to a content repository. Such solutions give authors control over how to structure the document, and are useful for longer documents.

Shorter items of content can also be annotated with metadata as part of publication process. Google introduced an online Structured Data Markup Helper that allows let authors tag different elements in their content.[221] The editors used in modern content management systems may offer similar capabilities natively, or through use of a plug-in. Tagging items via highlights is especially useful to add metadata to entities mentioned in the body of an article.

---

[220] "WYSIWYM", Wikipedia article,
  `https://en.wikipedia.org/wiki/WYSIWYM`
[221] Google Structured Data Markup Helper:
  `https://www.google.com/webmasters/markup-helper/`

Hardcoded Metadata

Newer content management systems will often allow the setting of metadata defaults when a basic content type is defined. For example, one could define the schema.org metadata that would accompany an event announcement. When an author fills in the information for the event, the appropriate metadata is generated. Such solutions work especially well when the content types are highly structured, and readily correspond to well-defined metadata elements. If the content is more loosely structure – for example, a story – the system will be able to generate only more basic metadata.

Appendix B. Glossary of Metadata Terms

Many definitions available for metadata terms tend to be formal, and are sometimes difficult to understand. They may use abstract terms in the definitions that have to be defined by other definitions. The definitions that follow try to be more conversational and helpful to novices, highlighting key points, rather than aiming for the comprehensiveness that an expert might expect. Accordingly, the definitions do not seek to indicate distinctions between related items, such as different schemas in use, or to cover everything that might be significant relating to a term.

Administrative Metadata

> Describes the history and provenance of the content.

API

> Application Programming Interface, a specification for making content available to other machines.

Attribute

> A dimension of an entity being described. Also referred to as a property.

Attribution Guidelines

A publisher's requirements about how content must be presented when other parties use the content.

Bad Metadata

(Informal term) Metadata with quality issues, because it is inaccurate (wrong or duplicative), imprecise, incomplete, or invalid (not machine-readable).

Categories

Represent available choices or varieties. They should be exhaustive and mutually exclusive.

Composite Values

Numeric data values that are composed of two or more dimensions, such as speed in kilometers per hour.

Content Item

A discrete piece of content that audiences consider meaningful and compete when viewing, such as an article, photo, video, or table. Compound content items are composed of more than one content item.

Content Model

Expresses the relationship between metadata attributes and various content types and components, indicating the circumstances when specific attributes are used.

Content Type

A framework defining the generic attributes associated with an item of content.

Controlled Vocabulary

A list of standardized terms, which must be used as values to describe attributes.

Creative Commons

A license framework indicating how people can reuse content

Crosswalk

Mapping different names for metadata properties and values used in different schemas, or by different organizations, to establish which are equivalent

Data Exchange Format

How metadata is encoded so that it can be used by different computer systems. Examples are XML and JSON.

Data Formatting

Rules governing the characters used in data values, such as abbreviations, punctuation, spacing and diacritics.

Data Structure

What entities and attributes can be used, and what the relationship is between broader and narrower entities. Also known as a schema.

Data Type

In computer terminology, the type of the variable associated with an object, which could be a string, floating point number, date, URL, Boolean, or other type.

Data Value

What descriptive values of an entity are allowed and expected.

Data Value Formats

How values in a description of an entity are formatted.

Descriptive Metadata

Metadata about the content indicating aspects such as the genre or thematic category, topics addressed, and entities mentioned.

Digital Assets

Generally refers to non-textual content, especially photos and videos.

Discrete Quantities

Quantities relating to discrete (separate and distinct) categories that are countable.

Dublin Core

A basic, general-purpose schema.

Enumeration

> A pre-defined list of valid values for an attribute, such as allowed names for days of the week.

Entity

> A specific thing, person, place, or concept addressed in the content.

Entity Resolution

> Determining whether entities identified as having different values in fact refer to the same entity.

Entity Type

> When specific entity instances share common attributes, they belong to the same entity type.

Expected Type

> In schema.org, the kind of value that must be used with a property in a description of an entity, either an entity type or data type.

Facet

> An dimension or aspect of the domain (the broad subject matter) discussed content, used to identify categories that should be described with metadata.

FOAF

> Friend of a Friend, an early metadata schema to express personal information, including relationships with other people.

Graph

> Structure that links together and reveals relationship between two things. Metadata supports development of **knowledge graphs** and **social graphs**.

Instance

> When a specific entity, such as a named person or place, can be positively identified within a content item.

Interval Quantities

> Quantities that are classified according to pre-defined numeric ranges.

ISO

> International Standards Organization, which is responsible for numerous standards

JSON

> A popular data exchange format used for web content

JSON-LD

> A data exchange format based on JSON used to express semantic metadata.

Lifecycle Metadata

> Retrospective and prospective information about dates relating to content item, such as date published, or date to be withdrawn.

Linked Data

> A series of best practices for publishing structured data on the web. Linked data facilitates the integration of content from different sources.

Machine Readable

> Ability of IT systems to identify and act upon entities, attributes and values correctly

Markup

> How specific metadata is encoded. A markup language or metadata markup format is how metadata is formatted in general, and is the same as a data exchange format.

Microdata

> An approach to putting structured data in HTML content. Often used with schema.org, a general-purpose data structure for web content, used for search engine optimization in particular.

Microformats

> A simple data structure to embed metadata in HTML, now largely superseded by schema.org

Metadata

> Data that describes a facet or aspect about a content item, or of a thing identified within the content.

Namespace

> A fixed online address (URI) that provides machine access to a specific public metadata schema.

Open Graph

> A metadata schema used by social networks such as Facebook.

Ontology

> A classification system for representing concepts, which groups items together based on common properties they share.

OpenRefine

> An open source tool for metadata clean up.

Proper Noun

> A thing that has a unique name, which is generally capitalized in English.

Property

> Same as attribute.

Proprietary Metadata

> When metadata does not follow common standards that support the exchange and sharing of the metadata.

Provenance Metadata

> Metadata relating to the creators, publication source, and reviewers or approvers of a content item.

Resource

> The subject being described in the metadata description.

Rights and Permissions Metadata

> Indicates copyright status of content, provide credits for content sourced externally, and indicate any restrictions on use or reuse of content

RightsML

> The Rights Expression Language, used for image rights.

RDFa

> A data structure that encodes semantic metadata within HTML.

RSS

> Really Simple Syndication, a format for web feeds that can be subscribed to.

Schema

> A framework for expressing the relationships between entities, and the attributes that entities have. Also known as a data structure.

Schema.org

> Popular general-purpose data structure or schema used by search engines to index web content

Semantic

> Used to refer to the meaning of content, especially for machines. Semantic metadata is machine-readable descriptive metadata.

Structured Data

> Another name for metadata, used to describe variables defined by a data structure.

Structural Metadata

> Identifies the role of a piece of content in the context of a larger content item.

Syntax

> How metadata is written in markup.

Taxonomy

> A hierarchical controlled vocabulary containing broader and narrower terms

Technical Metadata

> Defines the technical characteristics of a content item or file.

Translated Values

> When the value encoded in the metadata is converted for the audience into another scale (e.g., miles to kilometers) or into a relative value based on the user's context (e.g., distance from current location).

Transliteration

> How proper names for people and places in countries that don't use the Latin alphabet are rendered into Latin characters.

Toponym

> The name used to identify a location.

Triples

> A metadata pattern, which indicates metadata information in a three-part form of Subject - Property or Predicate - Object.

Use Metadata

> The incorporation of analytics information into administrative metadata, such as indicating the number of views for a content item to show to audiences or to support content delivery.

Units of Measure

> The scale used to indicate numeric quantities, including price, time, location, temperature, size and weight, as well as virtual measurements such as user or critic ratings according to stars or points.

Value

> The name, quantity or other variable associated with an attribute. See **Data Values** and **Data Value Formats**.

Variable Quantities

> Quantities that vary along a continuum, such as temperature, or average user rating.

Versions

> Different variations of a content item, that may reflect different revisions, languages, or formats.

Web content

> In this book, web content refers to any content produced for external audiences that is distributed through a digital channel (e.g., websites, mobile apps, APIs, kiosks, signage, appliances and wearable devices). Web content includes articles, audience-facing databases, graphics, audio and podcasts, video, and interactive widgets.

XML

A data exchange format, whose syntax is similar in appearance to HTML.

XMP

Extensible Metadata Platform, a schema for adding descriptive and administrative metadata to photos and other content objects.

YAML

A simplified markup language intended to substitute for JSON.

Appendix C. Resources

Data Exchange Standards

XML: http://www.w3.org/TR/REC-xml/

Microformats:
http://microformats.org/wiki/Main_Page

RDFa: https://www.w3.org/TR/rdfa-syntax/

Microdata: https://www.w3.org/TR/microdata/

JSON: https://tools.ietf.org/html/rfc7159

JSON-LD: https://dvcs.w3.org/hg/json-ld/raw-file/e582aaa9ee43/spec/latest/json-ld-syntax/index.html

Schemas

Creative Commons:
https://creativecommons.org/licenses/

Dublin Core:
http://dublincore.org/specifications/

FOAF: http://xmlns.com/foaf/spec/

GoodRelations:
http://www.heppnetz.de/projects/goodrelations/

Open Graph: http://ogp.me

RightsML:
https://iptc.org/standards/rightsml/

Schema.org: https://schema.org

XMP: http://www.adobe.com/devnet/xmp.html

Controlled Vocabularies and Data Formats

This book mentions a number of ISO standards, which are available at `http://www.iso.org/iso/home.html`. Unfortunately, ISO standards, unlike some other standards, are not free. Some standards are expensive. Fortunately, the core information about some of the most commonly used standards is available from Wikipedia and other public sources, which are listed when available.

BGN/PCGN (*Russian names*):
`https://en.wikipedia.org/wiki/BGN/PCGN_romanization_of_Russian`

ALA-LC (*Arabic names*):
`https://www.loc.gov/catdir/cpso/romanization/arabic.pdf`

E.123 (*Telephone numbers*):
`https://www.itu.int/rec/T-REC-E.123-200102-I/en`

GeoNames (*Geolocation ID & Coordinates*):
`http://www.geonames.org`

Getty's Thesaurus of Geographic Names:
`http://www.getty.edu/research/tools/vocabularies/tgn/`

GS1 Simple Product Listing™:
`https://www.gs1us.org/resources/standards/gs1-us-simple-product-listing-standard`

IPTC Media Topics:
`https://iptc.org/standards/media-topics/`

ISBN (*Book IDs*):
`http://www.isbn.org/faqs_general_questions`

International Standard Name Identifier:
`http://isni.org/how-isni-works`

International Standard Musical Work Code:
`http://www.iswc.org`

International Standard Recording Code:
`https://www.usisrc.org`

ISO 3602 (*Japanese names*):
`http://www.iso.org/iso/catalogue_detail.htm?csnumber=9029`

ISO 3166 (*Countries*):
`https://www.iso.org/obp/ui/#search`

ISO 4217 (*Currencies and Prices*):
`https://en.wikipedia.org/wiki/ISO_4217`

ISO 7098 (*Chinese names*):
`http://www.iso.org/iso/catalogue_detail.htm?csnumber=61420`

ISO 8601 (*Dates and Time*):
http://www.w3.org/TR/NOTE-datetime

Legal Entity Identifier (*Corporations*):
http://www.leiroc.org

Library of Congress Genres:
https://classificationweb.net/approved-subjects/1515.html

Open Researcher and Contributor ID:
http://orcid.org

Medical Subject Headings (MeSH):
https://www.nlm.nih.gov/mesh/

RFC 2822 (*Dates and Time*):
https://tools.ietf.org/html/rfc2822

Thomson Reuters Open PermID:
https://permid.org

UN/CEFACT (*Measurement units*):
http://www.unece.org/fileadmin/DAM/cefact/recommendations/rec20/rec20_rev3_Annex3e.pdf

UPC, EAN, JAN, GTIN-14 (*Product IDs*):
http://www.gs1.org/1/gtinrules/en/rule/264/new-product-introduction

UPU S42 (*Postal Addresses*):
http://www.upu.int/en/activities/addressing/s42-standard/compliant-countries.html

US Board on Geographic Names:
`http://geonames.usgs.gov/domestic/index.html`

Wikidata (*Measurement units*):
`https://www.wikidata.org/wiki/Special:ListProperties/quantity`

Useful Books

Deane Barker, ***Web Content Management: Systems, Features, and Best Practices***. O'Reilly, 2016.

- o An up-to-date, detailed discussion of how CMSs work.

Heather Hedden, ***The Accidental Taxonomist***. Information Today Inc., 2010

- o Background on how to create a taxonomy or controlled vocabulary.

Seth van Hooland and Ruben Verborgh, ***Linked Data for Libraries, Archives and Museums***. Neal-Schuman, 2014

- o While not focused on everyday web content, this book is excellent in discussing how to clean up metadata.

Kevin P. Nichols, and Donald Chesnut, ***UX For Dummies***. Wiley, 2014

- o Clear explanation of the relationship between content and user experience. Useful background to understanding how metadata fits into design activities.

Jeffrey Pomerantz, ***Metadata***, MIT Press, 2015

- A very good overview of metadata generally written for the non-specialist, though not focused on web content.

Airi Salminen and Frank Tompa, ***Communicating with XML***, Springer, 2011

- Provides a good explanation of how XML can be used to support metadata, without relying on a heavy focus on code. Not focused on web content

Leslie Sikos, ***Web Standards: Mastering HTML5, CSS3, and XML***, Apress, 2014.

- Approachable discussion of markup for web content. Covers some basics of HTML data formats, though it doesn't cover JSON or JSON-LD.

Ruben Verborgh and Max De Wilde, ***Using OpenRefine***, Packt 2013

- How to use OpenRefine to clean metadata.

Tools for Cleaning and Validating Metadata

JSON-LD Playground: `http://json-ld.org/playground/`

OpenRefine: `http://openrefine.org`

RDFa Play: `https://rdfa.info/play/`

Structured Data Linter: `http://linter.structured-data.org`

Structured Data Testing Tool: `https://search.google.com/structured-data/testing-tool`

Select Metadata-oriented Tools for Developers

Any23: `https://any23.apache.org`

"Library, a web service and a command line tool that extracts structured data in RDF format from a variety of Web documents"

RDFLIB : `https://github.com/RDFLib/rdflib`

"Python library for working with RDF", useful to convert data formats

RDFLIB.js: `https://github.com/linkeddata/rdflib.js/`

"Linked Data API for JavaScript"

Appendix D. About the author

Michael C Andrews is an American IT consultant currently based in Hyderabad, India.

He started working with online metadata as a technical information specialist at the US Commerce Department in the 1980s, and was among the first wave of people whose full-time job responsibilities focused on using the Internet to access and manage published content. For the past 15 years he has worked as a consultant in the fields of user experience and content strategy. He's worked as a senior manager for content strategy with one of the world's largest digital consultancies, and has advised clients such the National Institutes of Health, Verizon and the World Bank. He has lived and worked in the US, UK, New Zealand, Italy, as well as India.

Andrews has an MSc in human computer interaction from the University of Sussex in England, and a Masters with a specialization in international finance from Columbia University in New York. He also has a certificate in XML and RDF Technologies from the Library Juice Academy.

Index

Abstract attributes, 59
Actions, 64
 as entities, 53
Administrative metadata
 in Dublin Core, 185
Amazon, 198
APIs, 78, 80
Arabic, 290
Attributes, 57
 in XML, 127
Attribution guidelines, 99
Auditing metadata, 314
 process, 315
Authors, 31
Automation, 272
BBC, 324
Card sorting, 229
Categories, 61
 in taxonomies, 247
CEFACT, 291
Chinese, 289
Coding metadata, 328
Color, 295
Company names, 287
Compliance, 105
Composite values, 263
Conditional text, 43
Content assets, 50
Content credits, 98
Content formats, 84, 107
Content item, 48

Content Management
 Systems, 32, 78, 95
Content models, 70, 86, 94
Content restrictions, 98
Content reuse, 93
Content types, 94
Controlled vocabularies, 203
 external, 215
Coordination of terms, 257
Copyright, 96
Countries, 280
Creative Commons, 100
 framework, 102
Currencies, 292
Data formats
 and functionality, 270
Data linters, 329
Data structure. See Metadata schema
Data types, 202, 264
 in schema.org, 178
Dates, 278
DBpedia, 220
Delineators, 262
Descriptive metadata, 90
Digital assets, 113
Digital rights
 management, 103
Display taxonomies, 225

Dublin Core, 184
E.123, 283
Editorial metadata, 67
Entities, 52
　specifying a resource in schema.org, 173
Entity resolution, 208
Entity types, 54
　in schema.org, 178, 182
　multi-type entities, 182
Enumerations, 178
Exif, 106
Extensible Markup Language. *See* XML
External enumerations, 267
Facebook, 188, 194
Facets, 240
Field overloading, 312
FOAF
　example, 142
Format consistency, 256
Friend of a Friend (FOAF), 192
Geographic Names, 216
Geolocation, 281
　example, 282
Geonames, 282
Global Location Number, 283

Global unique identifiers, 207
GoodRelations, 192
Google, 169
Governance, 307
　and taxonomies, 235
　centralized, 211
　decentralized, 212
Graphs, 39
GS1, 211, 218, 283
GTINs, 284
Health-related information, 218
HTML Meta description example, 75
HTML5
　semantic elements, 137
Information architecture, 31, 225
International Tag Set, 88
Internationalization, 87
IPTC, 105, 211, 220
ISBN, 284
ISIC, 288
ISO 3166, 281
ISO 4217, 292
ISO 639, 277
ISO 8601, 278
iTunes, 114
Japanese, 289
jargon, 13

JSON, 148
  compared to XML, 152
  example, 151
JSON-LD, 153
  example, 155
Key, 59
Languages, 277
Legal Entity Identifier, 287
Lifecycle data, 85
Linked data, 167, 168
LinkedIn, 77
Location variants, 69
Markup
  errors, 311
Master data management, 115
Media Topics, 220
MeSH, 218
  example, 218
Metadata maintenance, 319
Metadata quality, 302
Metadata schema, 163
Metadata schemas
  implementation
    options, 197
microdata, 136
microformats, 131, 212
Microsoft, 73
Music metadata, 286
N3 syntax, 330

NAICS, 288
Namespaces, 167
Natural Language
  Processing, 33
Netflix, xviii
Normalization, 317
Numbers
  formatting, 259
Ontologies, 204
Open Annotations, 192
Open Data Commons, 103
Open Digital Rights
  Language, 103
Open Graph, 76
Open Graph protocol, 187
  example, 190
Open PermID, 288
OpenFace, 323
OpenRefine, 317
Personal names, 285
Personalization, 69
Photos, 323
Pinterest, 77, 190
Postal addresses, 280
Prices
  formatting, 292
Product architecture, 232
Product descriptions
  common elements, 36
Product information
  management, 116

361

Products= IDs, 284
Proprietary metadata, 167
  risks, 235
Propriety metadata, 230
Propriety names, 231
Provenance data, 85
Quality problems
  business risks, 305
Quantities, 62
RDFa, 141
  example, 144
Really Simple Syndication, 77
Real-time content, 326
Refactoring metadata, 316, 319
`rel` Attribute, 133
RFC 2822, 279
Rights Expression
  Languages, 100, 110
Rights metadata, 95
RightsML, 104
Russian, 290
S42, 280
schema.org, 169
  coverage, 175, 183
  example, 179
Scholarly HTML, 111
Search engines, 74
  use of schema.org, 171
Semantic metadata
  as a term, 109
Simple Product Listing, 218
SKOS, 250
Structured content, 22
Structured data, 21
Structured Data Markup
  tools, 332
Structured data testing
  tools, 140
Style guides, 255
Tag managers, 70
Taxonomies
  audience-facing, 224
  broader and narrower
    terms, 243
  business requirements, 231
  creating, 230
  enterprise, 223
Technical metadata, 105
Telephone numbers, 283
Terminology
  crosswalks, 228
  harmonization, 237
Text values, 206
Times, 278
Topics, 53
  as Content Type, 64
Transliteration, 289
Triples

in RDFa, 143
Turtle, 330
Twitter, 193
Units of measure, 265, 290
Universal Product Code, 285
Use metadata, 89
User experience, 6, 273
Values, 61
   duplication, 309
   inconsistent, 309
   missing, 308
   translated, 268
Video, 324
   microdata example, 139
   YouTube, 114
Wikidata, 221, 291
Wikipedia, 212
Workflow, 68, 105
Workflow automation, 88
WYSIWYM editors, 332
XML, 123
   example, 126
XMP, 282
XMP (Extensible Metadata Platform), 193
YAML, 330

Printed in Great Britain
by Amazon